2⁰⁰

THE RELUCTANT REFORMATION

THE RELUCTANT REFORMATION

ON CRITICIZING THE PRESS IN AMERICA

Lee Brown

University of Maryland

David McKay Company, Inc., New York

THE RELUCTANT REFORMATION

On Criticizing the Press in America

International Standard Book Number: 0-679-30258-1 (paper)
0-679-30257-3 (cloth)

Library of Congress Catalog Card Number: 74-76642

Manufactured in the United States of America

Design by Bob Antler

To my daughters,
Diana and Sydney

PREFACE

This is a book about criticism of the press; a small
volume for so large a subject. It was undertaken with
the notion that criticism is crucial and necessary if
the press is to serve the needs of a complex,
changing, and often troubled society.

Occasionally, this book is critical of the press,
and of the criticism of it; I hope with good and
sufficient cause. Its title is meant to suggest that the
press often has been slow to heed its critics,
reluctant to adopt the reforms that society constantly
requires of its press. Even so, few of our institutions
have improved so much in the past two decades. It
may be that demands have outstripped the present
capacity for change and improvement by a half step,
even a crucial half step. A free, responsible, and

responsive press cannot afford to be a half step behind because it is one of the cornerstones of the society it serves.

The first chapter attempts to relate theories of criticism to the contemporary press, to define the public interest relative to the press, and to discuss the role of criticism and the social responsibility of the press. Chapter 2 presents a concise history of press criticism, drawing upon its British origins and following the mainstreams of criticism to its current triumphs, traditions, and contradictions. Chapter 3 surveys the several distinct new (and some not-so-new) forms of press criticism. It focuses chiefly on experiments and applications in criticism and self-criticism. The fourth chapter is devoted to the revivals and recidivism that have attended proposals for a national press council, and to the function and purposes of the several forms of national councils. Chapter 5 summarizes the reasons necessitating press criticism, to suggest possible future developments, and to explain more completely the purpose of this book. The appendices, which speak largely for themselves, are included to suggest the ethical bases for press criticism and to present some widely differing experiments in criticism.

I am indebted to many in preparing this volume. I owe much to the newsmen and women with whom I worked for several years in Southern California. I also am indebted to those who served on the faculty of the School of Journalism of the University of Iowa between 1968 and 1970. I owe much to my colleagues at the University of Maryland.

Some friends deserve special acknowledgment for contributing to this study, particularly Richard W. Budd, Hanno Hardt, and Richard W. Lee. Linda J. Gemmrig and Margie L. Tivol offered useful suggestions and spent long hours in helping prepare the manuscript. While I alone am responsible for the contents of this volume, many have contributed to whatever merit it proves to have.

College Park, Maryland
April 1974

CONTENTS

ix

x Contents

THE RELUCTANT REFORMATION

1 POWER, THE PRESS, AND CRITICISM

Journalism and those media of mass communication
that are vehicles for it are social institutions of
immense importance to society. They gather,
process, and distribute news of the week, day, hour,
and even of the minute. As social institutions, the
media provide most of the information we receive.
Socially pervasive and physically ubiquitous, the
media also constitute a major American industry.
Individual units of the media are usually significant
economic forces in the communities in which they
are located, and the larger units contribute to and are
intricately involved in both regional and national
commerce. In the political sphere, the media
appropriately have been termed the "fourth branch
of government," an appellative describing

1

journalism's function as watchdog over and influencer of the three other branches. The media have power and influence in the social, political, and economic spheres of society. Because they supply us with so much crucial information, they are largely responsible for each person's perceived reality and his funded information.

The press informs us, entertains us, and educates us; but vast as it is, it is unique among our powerful social institutions in that it has no public franchises, has been granted no licenses, has no binding contracts for what it produces, and has been excluded from the major sociopolitical contract of American democracy, the Constitution. Freedom of the press is guaranteed by the First Amendment of the Bill of Rights, appended to the Constitution two years after ratification of the basic document in 1789.

Viewed historically, two developments advanced the press to such a position. First, the press preceded the establishment of the federal government during the colonial and Articles of Confederation periods. It had already developed germinal traditions of its own, had achieved at least some popular support, and had been used by the makers of the federal government to advance their own causes first during the struggle for independence from England and later in the fight for a federal system of government. It was an altogether different case in Europe where governments had existed since medieval times and were better able to impose regulations on the press during its infancy.

The second development was, simply, that neither freedom nor regulation of the press became major issues during the structuring of the government. Alexander Hamilton had argued for a free press in the Federalist papers published in the New York press as part of the campaign urging that state's ratification of the Constitution. Although experiences with authorities before the Revolutionary War taught the colonists that British practice fell short of English tradition, Hamilton's plea came in the spirit of John Milton's seventeenth-century argument that truth would always triumph over error in a fair encounter. The notion was that the press would provide the arena for conflicting views and needed to be free in order to maintain an open arena. Other questions of power seemed more important at the time the Constitution was written: How could the learned and the landed be protected from the common man? How could power be checked and balanced among the major divisions of the proposed government? How could states differing in size and population find equal representation? Should the several states be subordinated to a strong central government? How could the young nation establish itself among the community of nations? The Constitution thus defined the structure and execution of government without reference to the press, and the Bill of Rights defined the spirit of the new government with a single if crucial guarantee of freedom in the First Amendment, a recognition of principle and not power.

At least one reason for the omission of the press is that, at the time, the press was more venal than powerful. It was dependent almost wholly on patronage and was servile to its patrons. It indulged itself almost exclusively in political issues and was wildly partisan; smears, name-calling, distortions, character assassination, and malice were the rule rather than the exception. The irresponsible conduct of the party press canceled much of its power as a social force if not as a social irritant. It had little mass credibility as an institution, but achieved some popular stature through the notable contributors who used the press to advance their personal ideas and party causes.

No one could foresee the era of mass circulation and the alliance with business and commercial interests which began in earnest in 1833 with the establishment of the first of the penny papers, the New York *Sun*. It was an alliance that signaled the end of the party press; the penny papers deemphasized political issues in favor of detailed accounts of murders, trials, suicides, and accidents. The editors of the day invented sensationalism, which was to remain a principal feature of the metropolitan press well into the twentieth century. Similarly, it was impossible to foresee the industrial revolution and, particularly, the development during the 1850s of the high-speed rotary press and the stereotyping process that would transform the press from the hand craft of printers to a mass medium with a quantum increase of power.

The first newspaper venture in colonial America, *Publick Occurrences Both Forreign and Domestick*, was suppressed in Boston in 1690 after publication of a single issue. Subsequent newspapers were likewise suppressed, licensed, or permitted to publish only at the pleasure of colonial administrators. Early newspapers were reliant upon foreign news taken from English papers, essays, verses, personal letters, and whatever domestic information was available firsthand or could be plagiarized from other colonial newspapers. Exceptions were limited more to quality than to kind. One of them, the *New England Courant*, published by James Franklin, brother of Benjamin Franklin, opposed constituted authority in Massachusetts, not by confrontation, but by adopting the "snickersnee" style of comment popularized in England in *The Tatler* and *The Spectator*. The press had matured by the time of the Revolutionary War. It had divided between Tory and Revolutionary, and when hostilities broke out in 1775, few of the thirty-odd newspapers then in the colonies remained neutral. Following the war, newspapers grew in number and in frequency of publication. They also were strident in supporting the causes of the Federalists and the Republicans who were battling over the shape of the new government.

The arguments continued long after the shape was determined. Nine years later, a serious effort to regulate the press through federal law occurred during the administration of John Adams. The passage of the Alien and Sedition Acts of 1798 was in part an effort to preserve Adams's political party and the philosophies it represented. The acts had the indirect social effect of conferring a kind of legitimization on the press through political contract. Regulation was possible through judicial and legislative regulation, but the essential effect of the acts was censorship; it was a contract destructive of the freedom of the press.

The last of the four acts provided punishments of up to five years' imprisonment and a $5,000 fine for anyone convicted of bringing officers of the government into disrepute through writing or printing. Opposition to the acts became a major plank in Thomas Jefferson's campaign platform in the election of 1800. Jefferson, who had railed against "the falsehoods of a licentious press," nevertheless proved a champion for its freedom. The acts were allowed to expire after his election, and the few persons jailed under their provisions were set free.

Years later, Adams addressed himself to the increasing power of the press from the view of a man accustomed to power. The suppression of the Alien and Sedition Acts was long past, and the press was still growing and yet to come into its own. Adams wrote to a friend in 1815:

> If there is ever to be an amelioration of the condition of mankind, philosophers, theologians, legislators, politicians and moralists will find that the regulation of the press is the most difficult, dangerous and important problem they have to resolve. Mankind cannot now be governed without it, nor at present with it.

The regulation of its parts is organic in societies. In structuring governments and in developing institutions, societies have invented mechanisms and systems to distribute power so that balance, order, and, thus, survival may be achieved. When laws and traditions fail to order power, societies seek other ways to accomplish subordination. The job of society is to develop and maintain institutions which serve its best interests. "The first principle of a civilized state is that power is legitimate only when it is under contract."[1] This is a concept of immense importance in understanding journalism and the mass media in modern society as well as the need for criticism of the press.

The press represents both a paradox and a dilemma for contemporary society. The press serves best when it is free; but, free as it is, how can it be known that the press is serving? What assurance is there that the press (in its several forms, including broadcast) is responsible and that its performance justifies the guarantee of the First Amendment? The dilemma, simply, is one of devising a way to control without controlling.

In an era in which society has shown itself particularly suspicious of the power enjoyed by its several major institutions of government, it follows that the press, remote from direct societal control, should receive its share of disaffection. Most persons pay at least lip service to freedom of the press as an article of faith, but there is little evidence to indicate that this is much more than idle, tacit agreement. The maintenance of a free press has proved a preoccupation with its member persons and institutions, and often a chore for the judicial establishment. Rarely has press freedom been a popular issue, and this is only partly because there have been few incursions in press freedom to cause it to become a public or popular issue. At least one other reason is that the social contract between the press and society is only an implied one, and its provisions accordingly are vague. The practical distribution of power in any one-to-one exchange is asymmetrical, heavily weighted in favor of the press. If the press chooses, it usually may act without regard for effective reaction. An equal and viable exchange between the press and society, in any part or parts, is possible only if the press is willing. If power in a civilized state is legitimate only when it is under contract, there is an unavoidable lack of legitimacy about the place of the press in contemporary society. This is no less a dilemma for the press than it is for society.

One way of looking at the press in society has been to find purpose in function. That is to say that the press survives because society finds value in the services it performs. One sociologist has defined the function of the press in a four-part, widely accepted taxonomy:

—Surveillance of the environment, or the "watchdog" function, in which information concerning occurrences and events in the environment are collected and distributed.

—Correlation of the parts of society, including analysis, interpretation, evaluation, and editorial prescriptions for related behavior.

—Transmission of the social heritage from one generation to the next, particularly the preservation and imparting of social norms, values and beliefs to new generations; an educational function.

—Entertainment, activities, or content intended for amusement.[2]

Outlining the function of the press is useful for understanding performance, but more illuminating is the discussion of how the press ought to behave relative to its function. The most important recent statement on press behavior was issued in 1947 at the dawn of popular television, before the paperback-book boom, and at a time when newspaper editors and publishers apparently were particularly ill prepared for cogent criticism; to describe the reaction of the press fraternity as merely surly is more kind than accurate.

The Commission on Freedom of the Press, chaired by Robert M. Hutchins, then president of The University of Chicago, imported into the lexicon of press theory a new phrase: social responsibility. The commission was established in 1942 by Time, Inc. and Encyclopaedia Britannica, Inc., with a $215,000 grant. Its report, published in 1947, represents a significant modification of what has been called the libertarian theory of press performance. The commission specified that the press should:

—Provide a "truthful, comprehensive, and intelligent account of the day's events in a context which gives them meaning."
—Regard themselves as a forum for the exchange of comment and criticism, as a common carrier.
—Project a representative picture of the constituent groups in society.
—Present and clarify the goals and values of the society.
—Provide full access to the day's intelligence.[3]

These five requirements, the commission concluded, are what society is entitled to demand of its press. It amounts to a demand that the press in its several forms operate in the public interest even though its individual units continue in the private sector of the economy.

Useful definitions of the public interest are hard come by. Walter Lippmann's is as valid as any, and he described it as "what men would choose if they saw clearly, thought rationally, acted disinterestedly and benevolently."[4] His definition comes very close to the definition of "objectivity" in the handling of news, a concept that captured the journalistic conscience during the first quarter of this century along with a flurry of formal codes for the conduct of journalism and the mass media. It was the beginning of the end for the permissive tradition of hoax, fiction, and the sensationalism of "knee-jerk journalism" that characterized much of the American press since 1835. It didn't die easily, and it isn't wholly dead yet. Even so, concern for the public interest and what we now call the social responsibility of the press has captured the mainstream of journalism and is the pith of most of the criticism of the press.

The advent of radio, and the development of wire services, news magazines, and television emphasize the growth of the media during a period of unequaled growth of the nation. Today, America has more (and probably better) media units than any nation in the world. Even so, for all its technological, ethical, and educational advancements and resources, the press has not managed to keep abreast of the demands of society. An alternative description of the situation is that societal demands have exceeded the capacities for growth and change of many social institutions, including the mass media. It is ironic that the one institution that chose for itself the task of exposing the "feet of clay" of other institutions of society has discovered its own feet similarly mired, at least similarly mired in the judgment of what appears to be a large segment of contemporary society. In 1968, Wallace Allen, managing editor of the Minneapolis *Tribune*, said, "Public criticism of newspapers is the shrillest and most widespread I have seen in eighteen years. The public mood is uneasy, querulous, fearful." [5]

Similarly, according to a 1968 national poll conducted by Louis Harris, of nine out of ten Americans who say they read a newspaper regularly, a clear majority is convinced that the paper they read is "sometimes unfair, partial and slanted." [6] The Harris poll also indicated a growing distrust of television news reporting. M. L. Stein, writing in the *Saturday Review*,[7] reported what he saw as a sharp rise in public criticism of the press following the Democratic convention held in Chicago in August 1968. Norman Isaacs, writing in the *Bulletin* of the American Society of Newspaper Editors, reported about the mail he had received after his appearance on a National Educational Television program in rebuttal of Vice-President Spiro Agnew's speech criticizing television commentators in November 1968. He wrote that he was shaken because he never had experienced hate mail in such volume.[8]

In recent years, the press has not suffered from a paucity but rather a plethora of popular criticism from every sector of society. This is not lost on those who write, edit, and broadcast. Some newsmen are concerned that the press is losing the trust and friendship of its readers and viewers. If so, it would be a loss of catastrophic proportions for an institution that prides itself on public service.

Popular complaints do not make up the universe of criticism of the press. Sociology, political science, communication, and journalism professors fire off criticisms of the press with almost metronomic regularity, a regularity that serves to impeach the merit of their criticism in some instances and to mask its lack of merit in others. There is a kind of "sheer futility" about criticism, "especially for university teachers [when it becomes] merely an automatic method of acquiring merit, like turning a prayer-wheel." [9]

It is important to note that a critical attitude is not necessarily criticism. Carping and caviling on the one hand, or pointing-with-pride as an act of promotion or braggadocio on the other, is not criticism; criticism is an intellectual, cognitive activity with its own conceptual framework. Criticism should have "a structure of thought and knowledge existing in its own right." [10]

One of the smaller lessons of history is that usually it is folly to criticize the critics. Even so, criticism is as susceptible to being criticized as any other social activity. This is no less true of critics. To discuss the social function of criticism and critics also is to discuss what criticism ought to be. Since criticism is not necessarily more valid than the thing it criticizes, it must stand or fall on its own social value in a context of service to the public. Not all criticism is constructive, yet the generative aspect of criticism is where its principal social value may be found. Too often criticism is viewed—and occasionally is practiced—as a means to destroy something. Its most redeeming quality, however, is in its ability to generate improvement and to sustain the best of the thing being criticized.

One of the functions of criticism is social control

through social articulation, and one of its principal by-products is social legitimization. Criticism articulates when it modifies the practices of artists or professions and, at the same time, impacts popular taste by altering societal standards of acceptability and desirability. Criticism, particularly institutionalized criticism, is crucial to the conduct of several major forces in civilized societies. Ironically, the mass media themselves have become the principal institutions for criticism of art, the theater, films, literature, and music. Publicly conducted criticism is a major controlling agent of these several arts; through criticism, society extends suffrage and its acceptance of the arts frequently is defined through standards developed by professional critics. Criticism can be a means of societal control, and it can afford an implied social contract when no written one exists in law. It can articulate the standards of an art or profession with the values of society.

One crucial determinant is the level of discourse. Criticism should be the reasoned product of a reasonable mind or minds. It should function in and incorporate something of the definition of public interest already discussed: "what men would choose if they saw clearly, thought rationally, acted disinterestedly and benevolently." Criticism should aim at being helpful if it is to help. It should aim at a judgment instead of a censure. It should be sustained. Above all, the level of discourse must be maintained as a function of reason, not bias, whimsy, or self-interest.

Criticism should have cultural as well as social value. Northrop Frye, a critic of literature, has written:

> A public that tries to do without criticism, and asserts that it knows what it wants or likes . . . loses its cultural memory. . . . The only way to forestall the work of criticism is through censorship, which has the relation to criticism that lynching has to justice.[11]

Calls for more press criticism have come from journalists, but more appear to have come from the public and from those closely allied with the press as educators, students, or critics. In 1964, Louis M. Lyons, then curator of the Nieman Foundation for Journalism, Harvard University, observed:

> No other institution more requires constant and searching criticism, regardless of the hypersensitivity to criticism so often evidenced by too many of its proprietors. . . . The lack of any sustained criticism of so essential an institution as the press is a serious lapse in responsible relationships in a rational society.[12]

Robert J. Manning, before he became editor of the *Atlantic*, wrote: "The press today suffers from a bad case of complacency and self-righteousness and is noteworthy among all fraternities that perform public services for its lack of self-criticism." [13]

In 1970 the American Society of Newspaper Editors turned down a proposal to establish a national grievance committee to handle criticisms of substance. The association president had argued that the committee would be the "first national effort for self-examination by American Journalism," [14] but the directing board instead established a committee on ethics to review the organization's Code of Ethics and to respond to broad criticisms of newspaper performance.

This discourse raises questions that are crucial to any discussion of press criticism, and, at a different level of analysis, to any discussion of criticism. Who has the right to criticize? Why? Who has the obligation to be self-critical? Why? If not "who," then what kind of organization or organizations have such rights or such obligations?

The answers to some of these questions begin with a characterization of the relationship between the critic and his public. Hugh Dalziel Duncan wrote:

Criticism is a judgment, and, whether the critic functions as censor, reviewer, newsgiver, or reading analyst, he is doing so in terms of his responsibilities to some public and is telling his public how the author's creation threatens, sustains, or destroys that public's values.[15]

The standards and ideals embodied in criticism suggest the standards and ideals of the profession, as well as those of the public. Duncan also argued relative to the institutional posture of the critic that meaning must be explained not only to members of an institution but also to others outside it who may already be supportive or antagonistic.[16] He also raised the question of who has the "right" to criticize:

. . . it is very important to discover who is assigned the right to criticize; what institutions assume the guardianship of criticism; how these institutions defend their guardianship in competition with other institutions; how those who are to criticize are selected, trained, and supported; to whom criticism may be communicated; and on what occasions criticism is required.[17]

The discovery of who has the "right" to criticize the press is a discovery yet to occur, as is the discovery of who has the "right" to decide who has the "right." Each day's edition and each news broadcast obviously is susceptible to anyone who experiences it and who chooses to pass judgment. The press frequently has taken some refuge in the notion that its product is consumed by a universe of critics and that new or continued subscriptions or high viewer ratings indicate that a good job is being done, a position that avoids the moral obligation to be self-critical. If, as has already been observed, a critical attitude is not necessarily criticism, an uncritical attitude cannot be criticism.

In terms of guardianship of its right to criticize itself, the press has generally dealt with criticism from outside its membership by discounting it, ignoring it, or by counterattacking with what has sometimes been described as paranoiac fervor.

The discussion of what is and is not criticism implies a second question: What is or is not a critic? T. S. Eliot, discussing literary criticism, identified four kinds of critics: the professional critic (whose criticism is his principal title to fame), the critic with gusto (who is the mere advocate of the works he expounds), the academic-theoretical critic (the scholar or moralist who is apart from the things he criticizes) and the critic whose criticism is a by-product of his principal activity (the self-critic).[18] He believed the criticism of the self-critic to be the most authoritative.

Eliot's classifications of critics obtain as well to press criticism as to literary criticism. A fifth classification of press critic might be added to Eliot's original four. The emeritus critic (as opposed to critic emeritus) is the retired newsman, usually successful, who looks back upon a long career and criticizes the press from the security of retirement and professional respect.

Eliot observed that, in other types of criticism, "The historian, the philosopher, the sociologist, the moralist, the grammarian may play a large part." [19] This hardly can be contested in the area of press criticism. Fresh insights, sober analyses, and cogent, substantive criticisms have come from outside the parameters of the press. The Hutchins Commission, which included no member of the press, produced this century's most celebrated statement on social responsibility of the press. Unfortunately, at least at the outset, the celebrants included few members of the press.

One critic of the press, Herbert Brucker, in discussing the reaction of the press to the report of the Hutchins Commission, wrote:

> To this day there is a tendency among journalists to dismiss outsiders as incompetent to judge press

performance . . . the denigration of outsiders as
incompetent to measure press performance is, of course,
the argument *ad hominem*. This is a logical fallacy,
because what matters is the validity of what is said, not
who says it.[20]

Self-criticism is the most likely to be heard within the
profession, and at least one reason that it is more likely to be
attended to is that journalists expect it to contain substance
more pertinent than other kinds of criticism because the
practitioner should know the most about his practice.

Journalists correctly note that criticism of the press goes
on endlessly at different levels. Within the journalistic
establishment, criticism of journalism and the press occurs
informally at social gatherings and at press clubs. More
formally, it is conducted among staff editors at daily and
weekly news conferences, by individual news media of all
kinds, by wire and press association standing committees, at
the network level, at conventions, and in journals existing as
sounding boards for criticism.

According to Charles C. Clayton, a past president of
Sigma Delta Chi, a national society of journalists, the lay
public knows little of what goes on within the establishment
and finds the apparent lack of self-criticism and
self-regulation of the press difficult to understand. "Nothing
would do more to allay public suspicion of the press than
continuing and intelligent self-criticism," he wrote.[21]

Some critics disagree with the proposition that the press
is best able to judge itself. Among objections to self-criticism
are: the nature of any system tends to define the parameters
of possible criticism for those who would think critically and
limits the kinds of new answers possible; the opportunities
for whitewash are too great not to be taken advantage of;
and continued participation in an enterprise such as news
gathering is likely to reduce the vigor of self-criticism to a
level of mere self-interest.

Among others, Harry S. Ashmore, former editor of the *Arkansas Gazette* and long associated with the Center for the Study of Democratic Institutions, has consistently opposed the notion that the press can criticize itself. He wrote in 1966 that effective criticism can come only from persons outside of and independent of the media, and in discussing the reaction of the press to the Hutchins Report said:

> . . . in a curious way it became the special target of sensitive and frustrated men who privately recognize the media's grave deficiencies but feel constrained publicly to deny their existence. The experience of the past twenty years provides ample evidence to refute the specious arguments of the early days. Even those who still contend that the media are doing the best they can rarely argue that the best is good enough.[22]

When Ashmore's comments were published in the *Columbia Journalism Review* the following year, he was challenged by Arthur E. Rowse, a syndicated columnist on economic affairs. Rowse rejoined:

> . . . the fact is that the most effective criticism of the press has come and will continue to come—from within the press.
> The reason is simple: critics inside the press are the most knowledgeable and therefore the most likely to be heard by their confreres. . . . Most editors, I believe are ready, willing, and uniquely able to undertake considerable self-appraisal. And in my opinion they are doing an increasing amount of it. This is occurring wherever editors gather, and it should be fostered rather than ignored . . . newspaper editors are still the only people capable of appraising the performance of the press with any degree of success. Radio and television already are monitored by two forces that don't apply to newspapers: columnists and the FCC.[23]

The division of self-criticism from criticism of other derivation is not a "straw man" approach to the problem. Theoretically self-criticism should have a greater legitimizing or value-articulation potential than criticism from other sources. Its existence in the public domain should be its own statement of responsibility, and it should thus prove more gratifying to society. If this is a pragmatic value, there also are ethical ones. "The ultimate aim of all ethics is practical, for we desire moral knowledge in order to act on it." [24] Exploration of ethics relies on questions asking what ought I do? or what is my duty?

The point of this digression into the philosophy of ethics and morals is to underpin the assertion that the press has a moral and ethical duty to criticize itself. Brucker, in his "A Conscience for the Press," concluded similarly. He wrote:

> The conclusion seems inescapable. Newspapers and broadcasters had better do something themselves before some [government official or agency] does it for them—with a majority of the American public cheering [him or it] on. That is reason enough for the press to welcome a still, small voice of conscience, whose only strength is the newsman's own willingness to listen. But there is a better reason: It is right.[25]

Self-criticism may be seen here to have certain practical and ethical advantages in spurring improvement of the press, but the argument does not extend against criticism from other sources. The best criticism is likely to be a meld of criticism and self-criticism.

The moral and ethical behavior of the press should begin with values reflective of those of society at large. So should criticism and self-criticism. The media do not exist in a vacuum, but are a part of the society they exist to serve. Freedom presupposes responsibility, and it is threatened when other forces in and of society become convinced that the performance, or lack of performance, no longer warrants the protection. Affording freedom is not granting license, yet, in the libertarian tradition, the press has been often at odds with the values of society; sometimes it has created new values for society. In rendering service and disservice, the press stands popularly accused of failing to discriminate for itself which is which.

Characteristically, criticism of something occurs after the fact, that is, after the something has occurred. The standards and values underlying the criticism must be established before the fact and be visible to and known by the public, the critic, and those to be criticized. The arbitrary imposition of values after the fact is an invitation for rejection of criticism regardless of its intrinsic merit. The conceptual framework for the criticism cannot belong only to the critic, but its underlying values must be shared by the criticized. Criticism and self-criticism must acknowledge the presence of divergent values within the journalistic profession as well as the divergent values of a pluralistic society if it is to succeed.

Criticism must aim at the mediation of divergent values, it must be public in nature, and it must be based on known and preestablished values. That criticism must be public in conduct and based on known values is crucial to the legitimizing of the power of the press through social articulation. If criticism must serve where law does not, it must be accorded with similar public prominence. It must be open and widely communicated. Most important, it should be heeded.

The Canons of Journalism adopted by the American Society of Newspaper Editors in 1923, the radio and television codes, and the definitive statement of social responsibility in the Hutchins Report may meet the criterion of the necessity of having known and preestablished values. Yet, the Canons are becoming dated, the Hutchins recommendations paid little attention to broadcast media and are still eyed with suspicion in some sectors of the press, and there remains the persistent suspicion that only lip service is paid the broadcast codes, some provisions of which are so stringent and unnecessarily restrictive they deserve little more. Even so, criticism under the aegis of all these and similar statements of high purpose and moral intent only infrequently become public.

Moreover, the appraisals often are unorganized. Frequently they are mere recitations of trivia. Some are hopelessly diluted with altruism. At the other extreme, the criticism sometimes concerns problems so broad and of such great moment that reasonable response—the governing of individual behavior and conduct—is not facilitated.

There is and has been a broad area of self-critical discourse among journalists. Yet, the state of the art is such that the system is hardly self-correcting. One problem is that of the posture of the critic. Too much criticism begins with the notion that the press is either bad or good. Criticism should be critically positive. It is ineffective when it is motivated by a desire to prove something "good" or "bad."

Criticism should be realistic in that response is possible and guidance is offered. Its values must precede the criticism; both must be public. It should mediate actual and ideal values of the press and the public. It must be coherent and systematic relative to both.

Sylvan Meyer, editor of the Miami *News,* in criticizing the media appraisals of critic Marshall McLuhan, wrote of the plight of the newsman:

> Out of several major books and a host of articles and lectures, he ought to have some suggestions, not about the media in general, but about what I ought to do when I get to the office of a morning.[26]

Meyer's conclusion is suggestive of the aim of all ethics and descriptive of what press criticism ought to attempt. It

should provide journalists with something to act upon
leading to improvement of press performance.
Commensurately, open criticism also could provide a vehicle
for recognition of the improvements that have occurred,
particularly over the last two decades. Journalists proud of
the professional traditions of honesty, courage, integrity, fair
play, and literary craftsmanship may argue that education of
the public, and not criticism by it, is the best remedy for the
pervasive societal malaise that somehow has indicted the
press without regard for its improvement.

2 THE FABRIC OF PRESS CRITICISM: UNBROKEN THREADS

Critics and calumniators attended the press from its infancy in seventeenth-century England. Political partisanship, hoaxes, distortions, and often virulent advocacy among early printers and writers led to the foundations of a body of well-deserved criticism that was to follow the press across the Atlantic to the New World. The main themes of early criticism in England revolved around accuracy. First, there was a problem of the several new worlds opening to an England entering a period of enlightenment. Printers were quick to capitalize upon sensational (and often false) aspects of "surprizing Accounts of Monsters, Earthquakes, and floating Islands." The critical reaction was logical and distrustful. It urged the printing of domestic news, the truth of which could

21

more easily be ascertained. The editor of the *True Briton* wrote in 1723:

> The *True Briton* has already done some Service to the Publick, since he has provok'd the Mercenary and Hackney Scribblers of an abandon'd Faction to entertain the Town with *Domestic Abuses*, and to shorten the *Foreign Intelligence*, which generally used to fill their Papers. What they now seem to attempt, Every-Body can disprove, but their former Method of Entertaining us with Lyes from Abroad, could not so easily be confuted.[1]

A second critical theme developed, in part, as a natural progression from the first. In turning to domestic events, the editors were quick to seize upon scandal, brutality, rape, and other crimes for news. Then as now, "blood, sex and money" proved a successful formula for sales. Then as now, it was quick to be criticized by competitors as well as by men of letters.

A third critical theme involved advertising, centering on the deceptions of nostrum peddlers and quack physicians. Among men of letters who criticized early English advertising were Addison, Steel, and Defoe. Eighteenth-century England was popularly believed—at least by the English—to be "the best of all possible worlds." It was a time of an explosion of information and a broadening of horizons. It was a time for the ordering of things and for seeking order not only in England but in all of Europe, a quest that can be seen in the precise music of Mozart, the influence of rococo art, the calculus of Newton, even in the then current interest in Oriental gardening in England. The brash young press hardly fit the cultural mainstream, and the yet underdeveloped state-of-the-art richly deserved much of the stinging criticism it received. One historian's survey of criticism of the English newspapers of the time led him to conclude that inaccuracy, faking, coloring of news, triviality, venality, and advertising inconsistent with editorial proclamations of high purpose were targets of the bulk of press criticism.[2]

The character of the English press was transported to the New World with the equipment. Accordingly, criticism followed and acquired a character in keeping with the special problems printers and writers encountered in the colonies. There was an acute shortage of information, presses, type, paper, and skilled printers.

A new land was yet to be won. Criticism and self-criticism remained with the language of the adversary in the arena, and the themes remained relatively constant. George Washington, John Adams, and Thomas Jefferson were among prominent early Americans who lashed at the press at the close of the colonial era. John Ward Fenno, editor of the *Gazette of the United States*, wrote in 1799:

> The American newspapers are the most base, false, servile and venal publications, that ever polluted the fountains of society—their editors the most ignorant, mercenary, and vulgar automatons that ever were moved by the continually rusting wires of sordid mercantile avarice. . . .
> The newspapers of America are admirably calculated to keep the country in a continued state of insurrection and revolution.[3]

The editor of *Farmer's Museum*, of Walpole, New Hampshire, Joseph Dennie, took Fenno's characterization and expanded upon it the same year:

> Many of our American papers are not so valuable after being blackened and defiled by stupid printers and editors, as when immediately from the paper mill. Our domestic gazettes, when destitute of news, are not like the European journals, replete with entertainment and sound instruction. They are generally destitute of wit and originality. Indeed, a gross and slovenly system of

plagiarism prevails throughout. One wittol editor copies the nonsense of his simple brother; and false grammar, trivial remark, unimportant news, wire drawn poetry, and drowsy essays pass from hand to hand, and dulness enjoys a kind of newspaper immortality . . . the writer of this article can abundantly testify to the plagiarisms, mawkishness, dreariness, and gross folly of many of those weekly things, which profess to convey novelty and amusement to gaping reader. The fact is, there are three or four good papers published, upon which all the rest of us live.[4]

Fifteen years later, a similar criticism appeared in the first edition of the Boston *Daily Advertiser*, edited by Nathan Hale, the nephew of the Revolutionary War hero. Hale wrote in the "Editor's Salutatory:"

. . . it is only necessary to state that almost the total amount of the reading of at least one half of the people of this country, and of a great part of the reading of a large portion of the other half, is from the daily or weekly newspapers of the country. Many of these readers rely solely for information upon the amount afforded by a single paper. Thus the intellectual appetites of thousands of readers . . . are dependent for their periodical supply upon the frail understanding of a single editor.[5]

The partisanship of the early press endured along political lines until well into the nineteenth century. Even after the abandonment of the patronage system and the absolute alliance of newspapers with big business, the spirit of verbal warfare in the public print continued almost unabated until after the last great war between William Randolph Hearst and Joseph Pulitzer at the dawn of the twentieth century.

The advent of the penny press, the pursuit of mass circulation, and the entrenchment of advertising as the economic base from which newspapers would be published altered the course but not the character of self-criticism. As in the early epoch, self-criticism was against the opponent and could be called "self-criticism" only in the broadest sense of application. The party press battled for the loyalty of men's minds; since the penny press, the battle chiefly has been for dollars and that significant shift has been represented in the criticisms.

The following statement appeared in the Boston *Spectator* in 1836:

> They [the penny papers] are doing infinitely more to promote licentiousness and corrupt our youth, than they are doing good.
>
> No paper is more guilty in this respect, than the *Daily Times*, of this city. And it owes no little of its popularity to this very fault; and no one who regards good morals, should patronize it, (and we may say the same of the other penny papers).[6]

Since it is difficult to tell what is or is not criticism under any conditions, the passage of a century, and the unanswered original question of whether the author was speaking of morals or dollars combine to make the self-criticism issue cloudy.

The flamboyance of the penny press, particularly in the handling of sensationalized crime news, earned widespread criticism as well as widespread circulation. At least a part in this was played by powerful personalities such as James Gordon Bennett, publisher of the New York *Herald*. Characteristic of the atmosphere in New York was Bennett's account of a fist fight with a rival publisher, James Watson Webb, of the *Courier and Enquirer*. It was one of the first of Bennett's many feuds after beginning publication of the *Herald* in 1835. He reported that Webb attacked him on Wall Street first by pushing him down some steps and then "fighting with a species of brutal and demoniac desperation characteristic of a fury." Bennett reported he struck Webb "a blow in the face which may have knocked down his throat some of his infernal teeth for anything I know." [7] It was not an unprecedented occurrence, and the incident serves to illustrate one aspect of press self-criticism of that era.

Another aspect of press criticism aimed at the spectacular penny papers centered around crime coverage. Charles Dickens found it so sensationally odious in 1843 that he characterized one of his fictional hero's first impressions of New York with:

> "Here's this morning's New York *Sewer*!" cried one. "Here's this morning's New York *Stabber*! Here's the New York *Family Spy*! Here's the New York *Private Listener*! Here's the New York *Peeper*! Here's the New York *Plunderer*! Here's the New York *Keyhole Reporter*! Here's the New York *Rowdy Journal*! Here's all the New York papers! Here's full particulars of the patriotic locofoco movement yesterday, in which the Whigs was so chawed up; and the last Alabama gouging case; and the interesting Arkanses dooel with Bowie knives; and all the Political, Commercial, and Fashionable News. Here they are! Here's the papers, here's the papers!" [8]

Most journalism history focuses on the giants, a focus that necessarily imposes a major constraint on a review of criticism and press self-analysis. In a different perspective, considerable sophistication may be seen in Josh Billings' tongue-in-cheek advice to correspondents which appeared in the Virginia City Montana *Post*, June 1, 1867:

> No notis will be took of letters that haint got no postage stamp into them.
> Write only on one side of the manuskript and don't write much onto that.
> Don't send a manuskript unless you can read it yourself after it gets dry.

We pay, all the way up the hill, from ten cents to one dollar for contributions, according to heft.

Settlement made promptly at the end of the next ensuing year.

The highest market prices pade for awfull raleroad smashes and elopements with another man's wife.

Your remarks might possibly lead one more man to think as you do, and we don't want our collums held responsible for increasing the number of phools.

The world has already got more phools than there is any need of.[9]

As individualistic as Billings or Dickens himself were the great personal journalists of the middle and late 1800s. Among them were James Gordon Bennett, Henry Watterson, Horace Greeley, Isaac Hill, and Francis P. Blair. Their retirements from active journalism, particularly the deaths of Bennett and Greeley, led Samuel Bowles of the Springfield (Mass.) *Republican* to chronicle the passing of the old and the ringing in of what he saw as a new era. He wrote in 1872:

Their personality was the necessity of their creative work; it could not be suppressed by types and ink; but they have no successors, because there is no call for them,—the creators have given place to the conductors; and henceforth, American Journalism, in its best illustrations, will exhibit its outgrowth both of Partyism and Personalism.

It will become a profession, not a steppingstone; and a great journal will not longer be the victim of caprice and passion, or the instrument of the merely personal ambition, of its chance writer or conductor. Its traditions, its conscience, its responsibilities and its constituency will assume their appropriate powers over itself; and instead of a man, called to direct and contribute to its columns, importing himself into it, the paper will import itself into him.[10]

Bowles' insight was less than prophetic. The century was to march to its end keeping quick-time with the vicious newspaper war waged by Hearst and Pulitzer. This last of many great news duels—certainly to become the most celebrated—was fought in an atmosphere of unparalleled sensationalism and unchecked irresponsibility.

Edwin Godkin, editor of the prestigious weekly *Nation*, criticized with insight the period's journalism in 1894:

> But with a villainous press—venal and silly—and a somewhat frivolous and distinctly *childish* public, it is difficult to be sure of more than a few years [of good government]. I know of no good influence now which is acting on the masses, and the practice of reading trivial newspapers begets, even among men of some education, a puerile habit of mind.[11]

Two years later Godkin again was to attack what he saw as the puerility of the press, and wrote:

> What is wanted in the way of reform is mainly maturity, the preparation of the paper for grown people engaged in serious occupations. Gravity either in discussing or in managing our affairs is fast vanishing under the journalistic influence. We laugh over everything; make fun of everybody, and think it will "all come out right in the end," just like ill-bred children who hate to have their games interrupted.[12]

Godkin's criticism, however, was to be of no avail. According to Emery and Smith:

> By 1900 about one-third of metropolitan dailies were following the yellow trend which the *Journal* had set in New York. It was another 10 years before the wave of sensationalism subsided, as it had before, and newspapermen concentrated on intelligent use of the devices which had marked its rise. . . .[13]

The twentieth century brought the era of the muckrakers, and some newspapers and many magazines numbered among the front runners. Although the muck was raked from the general posture of defending the rights of the people, or the "little man," the trend represented a more or less natural shift from the highly exploitative yellow journalism that preceded it. The sensationalism remained, but the professional posture now bathed itself with altruism.

Novelists such as Frank Norris (*The Octopus* and *The Pit*) and Theodore Dreiser (*Sister Carrie* and *The Financier*) joined magazines such as *McClure's, Collier's, Munsey's,* and the *Saturday Evening Post* in the attack on big business and against what were regarded as the social injustices and inadequacies of American economic and political life.

The muckrakers reaped a harvest that had been sowed by the avarice and excess of more than fifty years of industrial revolution. No major industry escaped the scathing pens of the muckrakers, and the press was not an exception. Nor should it have been. Sensationalism, yellow journalism, and hoaxes were among the most conspicuous characteristics of American journalism through the last half of the nineteenth century. At the close of the century, deliberate overstatement in headlines was common and accepted practice in many city rooms, as was the practice of reporters and editors in supplying for news stories "the missing materials from his inner consciousness, drawing much upon his memory or his imagination." [14] One thoughtful assessment of press criticism appeared in 1924, toward the end of the muckraking period, looking backward at the performance of the press during and since the "yellow journalism" zenith of the 1890s. The press was being criticized for materialism and bowing to advertisers in return for advertising patronage, for manufacturing news through hoax and falsification, for coloring the news in the pursuit of sensation, for suppressing news to serve special interests, for the lack of editorial leadership, and for not establishing adequate professional standards for journalists.[15]

Others were less gentle with the press. Upton Sinclair's *The Brass Check* (1919) and Oswald Garrison Villard's *Some Newspapers and Newspaper-Men* (1923) depicted a cowardly press servile to exploitive capitalism and big business. Sinclair wrote, addressing himself to newsmen:

> . . . you who take the fair body of truth and sell it in the market-place, who betray the virgin hopes of mankind into the loathsome brothel of big business.[16]

Sinclair proposed legislation to prevent any story from being published that had not been approved by the principal subjects, as well as a mandatory retraction law. He also proposed that the press be put under public ownership.[17]

Members of the press were mindful of the clamor, and their own activities during the first twenty-five years of this century brought forth a spate of codes and statements of ethical standards.

The earliest code of ethics to be adopted by any association of journalists in America, the Kansas Code of Ethics, was adopted in 1910 by the Kansas Editorial Association. It was heavily oriented toward advertising policy, an orientation suggestive of the editors' sensitivity to the rising clamor against advertising, particularly false or misleading advertising.[18]

In 1911 *Printer's Ink* drafted a model statute about truth in advertising and the following year the federal Newspaper Publicity Law required that advertisements should be labeled as such.[19]

Following World War I, the Missouri Press Association in 1921, the South Dakota Press Association and the Oregon State Editorial Association in 1922, and the Washington State Press Association in 1923 adopted codes of ethics.[20]

In 1913, Ralph Pulitzer established the Bureau of

Accuracy and Fair Play of the New York *World* to investigate reader complaints and to order corrections when appropriate, and by 1924, the Detroit *News* employed an "editorial secretary" to perform a similar function.[21]

By 1924, Nelson A. Crawford was able to collect editorial codes from eight individual newspapers: the Brooklyn *Eagle*, the Springfield (Mass.) *Republican*, the Springfield (Mass.) *Union*, the Detroit *News*, the Sacramento *Bee*, the Seattle *Times*, the Kansas City *Journal-Post*, and the Marion (Ohio) *Star*.[22]

Of these codes, however, some were merely narrow-guage guidelines. The Seattle *Times*, for example, devoted seven of eight sections to the regulation of news content and language referring to sex under the initial admonishment, "Remember that young girls read *The Times*." Use of "rape," "adultery," "indecent exposure," "incest," and "assault" was prohibited.[23]

In 1923 the American Society of Newspaper Editors adopted its code of ethics, the Canons of Journalism. All the association codes, including that of the ASNE, were either unenforceable or not enforced with vigor. Even so, their existence represented some articulate if ostensibly impotent examples of implicit self-analysis.

Proof of the weakness of the Canons of Journalism was not long in coming for the ASNE. In 1924, the issue was raised whether the society should censure and perhaps expel Frederick G. Bonfils, co-publisher of the Denver *Post* and a society member. Bonfils was accused of accepting a payoff of $1 million in cash and oil options in exchange for not carrying news stories involving the Teapot Dome oil field. The ASNE ordered an investigation, but Bonfils was never censured. The society's members disagreed on interpretation of the Canons, particularly on whether the articles enabled the body to punish a member. Bonfils finally resigned and the Bonfils matter was allowed to die. In 1932, after years of debate and study, the ASNE adopted a compromise amendment providing for suspension or expulsion, but only after laborious due process proceedings had been completed with full right of reply for the accused.[24] No member has been censured under this provision.

The Bonfils affair became the theme of *Timberline* (1933), a book by Gene Fowler, which, in part, was critical of press ethics and the manner in which Bonfils was not censured. There were other criticisms of the press in the 1930s, most of them based on a broader attack. Robert Benchley, writing under the pseudonym "Guy Fawkes," wrote "The Wayward Press" column in the *New Yorker*. George Seldes and Heywood Broun also became prominent critics of the press, and Seldes produced a weekly newsletter, *In Fact: An Antidote for Falsehood in the Daily Press*, and wrote several books critical of the press. Among these were: *You Can't Print That* (1929), *Freedom of the Press* (1937), and *Lords of the Press* (1938).

Beginning in June 1933, and ending in December 1934, *Journalism Quarterly* published a six-part series on "Measuring the Ethics of American Newspapers: Spectrum Analysis of Newspaper Sensationalism."

The 1920s and 1930s also saw the rise of magazines as critics of radio as well as newspapers, although the critical focus remained on the latter. The *Nation, American Mercury, Commonweal, New Republic*, and *Atlantic Monthly* were among magazines frequently carrying critical evaluations of the state of American journalism; some of the analyses were written by practicing journalists.[25]

One study of criticism of the press in magazines during the period 1900–1939 enumerated and annotated 506 articles appraising or criticizing the press in general, the press as a social institution, the press as business, the newspaper in particular, the periodical press, radio, the news services, and press personalities. The study shows that peak periods of press criticism in magazines occurred in 1911 when one of the major themes was the decline of yellow journalism; in 1914, when wire service performance at the outset of World War I was an issue; during 1917–18, when the Espionage Act was thought to be a possible infringement of a free press; during 1923–28, when ethics of journalism, codes of ethics, the invasion of privacy, and the tabloid press were of current interest; and, during 1934–38, when the formation of the American Newspaper Guild (1934), the proposal to license newspapers under the National Recovery Act, privacy, press ethics, and sensational crime coverage were matters of currency. Other critical themes during the period included commercialism and advertising, censorship of the press, consolidation of the press, falsified news, sensationalism, and suppression of news.[26]

It was also a period for continuing the battle against advertising. The focus of the fight in the 1930s was over false and misleading advertising, but it also generated questions about the social or economic necessity of any advertising. Advertising was accused of being an uneconomic if not baleful influence upon society.[27] Among the authors who criticized advertising, and were criticized by advertisers, were Walter Lippmann, Thorstein Veblen, Sinclair Lewis, Sumner Slichter, Robert S. Lynd, and Gilbert Seldes.[28]

The reaction to the onslaught against advertising is well characterized by John Long, one of the founders of Newspaper Managers, Inc. Long, in discussing his related role in founding National Newspaper Week, wrote:

It goes back to the election of Franklin Roosevelt the first time and his crafty selection of The Press as his whipping boy; to the wave of insidious and pernicious propaganda of the Party Line that inspired leaders in high places to decry the venal press and even to poison our school textbooks with communistic tripe about advertising being an economic waste. The Whipping Boy took it standing up and Mr. Franklin Roosevelt became the first President of the United States ever to try actually to LICENSE the newspapers under the guise of the Blue Eagle of the National Recovery Act.

Then was born Newspaper Week in California to fight fire with fire, propaganda with propaganda, and might the best man win! I believe the best man won. The newspapers were not licensed; they again have the confidence of the people.[29]

The most succinct and complete summary of press criticism during the first three decades of the twentieth century is appended to George Seldes' *Freedom of the Press* (1937). Attributed to Carl W. Ackerman, the late dean of the Columbia School of Journalism, the criticisms bore strong vestiges of the consumer protectionist movement that was particularly ardent during the depression years of the 1930s. Ackerman's "The Nineteen Charges Against the Press" reflected well the depression, and the social and economic revolution of Franklin Roosevelt's New Deal which impacted press criticism as it did most other activities of the era. It pointed out, in particular, one of the enduring dilemmas of the press—that making money by publishing a newspaper is not necessarily compatible with telling all the truth all the time.

Ackerman wrote:

The Nineteen Charges Against the Press

1. That the newspaper standards are determined by circulation. The press gives the public what it wants, rather than what the public needs.
2. The newspaper violates the individual right of privacy.
3. Financial news is promotional rather than informative.
4. News values are often superficial and trivial.

5. Most reporters are inaccurate when reporting interviews.
6. Newspapers do not lead in public affairs, but follow the leadership of organized minorities.
7. Newspapers make heroes of criminals by romantic accounts of gang activities.
8. Headlines frequently do not correctly reveal the facts and the tenor of the article.
9. Newspapers are interested primarily in day by day developments and do not follow through to give the reader a continuous and complete account of what is happening.
10. Weekly newspapers are subservient to local political machines.
11. The press utilizes its freedom as a license to exploit policies which make for circulation rather than for service.
12. The press is not sincere in its attack upon special privilege because it accepts a subsidy from the Post Office Department.
13. The basic fault with the press is its ownership; that the press cannot be impartial and true advocate of public service so long as its owners are engaged or involved in other businesses.
14. News and photographs are sometimes falsified.
15. Many men and women hesitate to express their real opinion to the press because of the uncharitable attitude of editors toward criticism and because of their fear of retaliation.
16. In reporting Sunday sermons and religious meetings, the press seeks sensation rather than knowledge.
17. Corporations, private and public organizations, are compelled by self interest to maintain publicity departments to insure accurate reporting of their affairs and policies.
18. The press over-emphasizes irrational statements of public officials, particularly members of Congress.
19. In all civilized countries at present newspapers exist for the purpose of concealing truth.[30]

An obvious question is generated by Ackerman's nineteenth charge: Is this the point of the cynic or the question of the critic? Whichever, the answer is lost, and perhaps well lost, in the complicated history of press criticism. Four years after Ackerman's bill against the press appeared in Seldes' book, Bruce Bliven published his own list of indictments of the press. Bliven by then had been a press critic for more than thirty years, and the magazine he edited, the *New Republic*, had featured articles critical of the press for a like period of time. Bliven wrote:

1. The American Press Is the Best in the World.
2. The American Press on the Whole Is Improving.
3. Censorship by Publishers Is Worse Than That by Advertisers.
4. Newspapers Are Edited by Business Men.
5. Monopoly Is a Grave Danger in the Press.
6. There Is a Dangerous Tendency Toward Standardized and Syndicated Material.
7. The Middle Class Is Overrepresented in the Press.
8. Journalists and Papers Get Old, Fat and Timid.
9. In Technology There Is Hope.
10. We Get About What We Deserve.[31]

Bliven's indictments were reprinted in *The Newspaper and Society* (1942). The chapter began with a preface that could have been written thirty years later and still be as pertinent. The authors asked:

Can you believe what you read in the newspapers? A body of criticism, too huge to have been missed by the least erudite reader, has slowly accumulated through the years against the press for its inaccuracy, until it has actually become "the thing to do" to say that you can't believe what you read in the newspapers. This statement can be lightly tossed off, and it is usually popular wherever it is made, because it makes both speaker and listener feel superior to the men and women who publish those same newspapers.

But, can you believe what you read in the newspapers? . . . That question at a stroke lays bare the heart of the biggest problem concerned with the press. Hence, it is the accuracy of the facts as gathered by the newspapers themselves that is brought up for questioning here.[32]

The criticisms of Ackerman and Bliven marked the end of an era of criticism. After the outbreak of World War II, rationing slowed the consumer's movement against advertising, as the markets became sellers' markets. Voluntary censorship by the press in the interests of national security ended some criticisms of the press and made others irrelevant. The interests of the nation were turned toward survival and to the war abroad.

The U.S. Office of Censorship, created December 19, 1941, established a code for voluntary censorship among media covering the war abroad and the war effort at home. According to Mott, "The patriotic intention of editors and publishers and the extreme pressure exerted by the general backing of the programs by press and public made penalties for infractions unnecessary." [33] Internal critics of the press pointed with pride to the manner in which both radio and newspapers observed the rules of the game.

There were several notable exceptions. In one of them, the Associated Press suspended and finally dismissed Edward Kennedy, the AP chief on the Western front, after he broke the pledge to wait for the "official release" of the signing of the German surrender. Kennedy said he radioed the news only after it had been broadcast in Germany, Denmark, and England. But fifty-four newsmen in Paris signed a statement charging Kennedy with committing "the most disgraceful, deliberate, and unethical doublecross in the history of journalism." Kennedy later was reinstated as an official war correspondent by Supreme Headquarters in the European Theater of Operations. His premature release had beaten the presidential announcement of the German surrender by a day, but the occurrence brought bitter debate among the press.[34]

Another incident involved a hoax. A United Press flash stated two days before Japan's capitulation: *President has just announced that Japan has accepted the surrender terms of the Allies.* All UP wires carried notice of the flash to subscribers, but the "kill" was made three minutes after the original message was received. UP offered a $5,000 reward for information leading to the conviction of the hoaxer, but he was never discovered. No newspapers carried the flash, but some radio stations did in bulletin form.[35]

Five years after *The Newspaper and Society*, the report of the Hutchins Commission was published in 1947. Although it was to alter the language of press criticism by introducing the concept or at least the phrase of "social responsibility of the press" into it, its indictment of the press bore major similarities to preceding indictments.

The commission concluded that freedom of the press is in danger for three reasons: as the press became an instrument of mass communication, public access became more limited; those who control the media have not provided a service adequate to society's needs; and those in control of the media have engaged in practices which society condemns and thus have invited control by society.

The commission further specified by concluding:

These needs are not being met. The news is twisted by the emphasis on firstness, on the novel and sensational; by the personal interests of owners; and by pressure groups. Too much of the regular output of the press consists of a miscellaneous succession of stories and images which have no relation to the typical lives of real people anywhere. Too often the result is meaninglessness, flatness, distortion, and the perpetuation of misunderstanding among widely scattered groups whose only contact is through these media.[36]

Except for the concept of a finite social responsibility, the content of the Hutchins Commission Report represented a modification more than a break in the tradition of press criticism that preceded it. The coherent style in which its criticism was cast, its positive proposals, the unquestionable stature of commission members, and the power of expression in it gave the report nearly as much impetus as did the shocked reaction of the press to the idea of the national press council it proposed.

Hard on the heels of the Hutchins Commission arrived the social scientist, newly interested in the mass media, an advent that was to contribute a major chapter to press criticism.

If newsmen have assumed the existence of the press a "good thing," this cannot be said of the criticism of social scientists. Often, the presumption underlying their press criticism has been that the press is a "bad thing." According to William Stephenson, a social scientist at the University of Missouri:

Social scientists have been busy, since the beginnings of mass communications research, trying to prove that the mass media have been sinful where they should have been good. The media have been looked at through the eyes of morality when, instead, what was required was a fresh glance at people existing in their own right for the first time.[37]

For the newsman committed to the belief that his involvement was with a "good thing," the suggestion, even if only by implication and however covertly offered, that the press really was a "bad thing" accounts for out-of-hand rejection of many criticisms that could have made a positive contribution to the performance of the press.

The tone of the emergent criticism of the social scientist is suggested by Charles R. Wright's summary of an earlier work by Paul Lazarsfeld and Robert Merton. Wright wrote:

> First, many people are alarmed by the mass media's ubiquity and potential power to manipulate Man for good or evil. The average person feels he has little or no control over this power. Second, some people fear that economic interest groups may use the mass media to insure public conformity to the social and economic *status quo,* minimizing social criticism and weakening the audience's capacity for critical thinking. Third, critics argue that the mass media, in accommodating large audiences, may cause a deterioration of aesthetic tastes and popular cultural standards. Finally, some people criticize the mass media as having nullified social gains for which reformers have worked for decades.[38]

Even this was not a great departure from the criticism that preceded it. It still was a consumer-oriented criticism except, with Hutchins and the social scientist, the focus shifted from materialism and the consumer's pocketbook to the consumer's mind and the publisher's sense of social consciousness. But the suggestion of social omnipotence of the press, particularly an omnipotence wielded by a capricious, whimsical, self-serving power catering to the mob, makes the criticism vulnerable to Stephenson's caveat of attempting to prove the media sinful. Yet, the record shows that social scientists were more in than out of the mainstream of press critics in this.

A criticism with less formal expression is that of the intellectual. Writing in *Daedalus* in 1960, Leo Rosten presented what he saw as the critical posture of the intellectual relative to the media. He wrote:

> A great deal of what appears in the mass media is dreadful tripe and treacle; inane in content, banal in

style, muddy in reasoning, mawkish in sentiment, vulgar, naive, and offensive to men of learning or refinement.[39]

Rosten also outlined the principal complaints of the intellectual about the media:

1. The mass media lack originality.
2. The mass media do not use the best brains or the freshest talents.
3. The mass media do not print or broadcast the best material that is submitted to them.
4. The mass media cannot afford to step on anyone's toes.
5. The mass media do not give the public enough or adequate information about the serious problems of our time.
6. The aesthetic level of the mass media is appalling; truth is sacrificed to the happy ending, escapism is exalted, romance, violence, melodrama prevail.
7. The mass media corrupt and debase public taste, they create the kind of audience that enjoys cheap and trivial entertainment.
8. The mass media are what they are because they are operated solely as money-making enterprises.
9. The mass media are dominated—or too much influenced—by advertisers.
10. The mass media do not provide an adequate forum for minority views—the dissident and unorthodox.[40]

The plight of the intellectual unfulfilled by the media is not one unrecognized by the press, or at least by some sectors of it. For example, Bernard Kilgore, editor of the *Wall Street Journal*, was quoted in 1965 by *Newsweek* as remarking: "The newspaper of the future must become an instrument of intellectual leadership, an institution of intellectual development—a center of learning."[41]

To which *Newsweek* added:

That is lofty language, especially on the ear of a profession that takes a crusty pride in its habitual cynicism. Yet aspiration, however lofty, is surely one indispensable tonic for what ails the American newspaper. Typically, it is the best newspapers that are now most concerned with raising their sights. That should be a useful clue for the editors and publishers whose papers need improving most.[42]

Most of the other critical themes originating from outside the press also are shared by criticism emerging from within it. Lester Markel, Sunday editor of the New York *Times*, for example, produced his own five-point indictment of the press in *Harper's Magazine* in 1962. Its points strike notes by now familiar. He wrote:

1. Many, too many, American newspapers are media of entertainment rather than of information.
2. The newspapers, for the most part, are failing to make the important news understandable.
3. The newspaper has lost much of its prestige as a leader of public opinion.
4. The newspaper industry does a scant job of editorial research and self-analysis.
5. Training for journalism and pay to newspapermen are inadequate.[43]

Although recent self-criticism of newspapers by newspapers has been limited to only a few of the nation's papers—among them the New York *Times*, the *Wall Street Journal*, and the *National Observer*—some of the analyses in them have been hard-hitting and convincing. The *Wall Street Journal* ran an unsigned story in July 1967, and in over one hundred column inches, named names, newspapers, and places involving the most questionable professional ethics and practices. In part, the *Journal* reported that the buyer who "expects a dime's worth of truth every time he picks up his paper often is short-changed." The *Journal* made several substantial points:

—No newspaper can be sure that all of its staff can resist the blandishments of special interests who seek omission or distortion of the truth.

—Trouble often starts at the top when a publisher dictates policies designed to aid one faction or attack another.

—Some publishers have increased the pay of newsmen which, with policy statements about accepting gratuities, has narrowed the parameters of unethical behavior.

—Some publishers establish policies designed to aid one group or another; other publishers strive to report the news fairly and impartially and have raised salaries and established rules that promote ethical reportorial behavior.

—Newspaper ethics often fall short of "ethical purity," but they are improved for the most part.

—Newspapers should continue to resist outside pressures. Many don't because of low salaries—they tolerate practices incompatible with editorial independence and objectivity.[44]

At the 1966 convention of the Associated Press Managing Editors, J. Edward Murray, managing editor of the *Arizona Republic*, delivered a paper, "The Image of the Newspapers," [45] and identified three particular kinds of critics of the press. The identification came partly as the result of a questionnaire Murray had mailed to critics of the press.

He found "the woods full of critics, and a great deal of their criticism should be taken seriously." Specialists, he reported, find the press shallow and simplistic. The Berkeley Generation, the second category of critic, finds the press "old and tired and married to a lousy *status quo*." Murray's final type of critic was described as Idealists, Reformers, Utopians. This type, Murray said, finds the press timid, conformist, lacking in original thought and leadership, and failing in its educational role.[46]

The following year, A. H. Raskin of the New York *Times*

wrote his own criticism of the press and, in suggesting one possible remedy, proposed a solution that was to become a reality on some newspapers. Raskin wrote:

> The real long-range menace to America's daily newspapers, in my judgment, lies in the unshatterable smugness of their publishers and editors, myself included. Of all the institutions in our inordinately complacent society, none is so addicted as the press to self-righteousness, self-satisfaction and self-congratulation.[47]

Raskin urged that every paper needs a "Department of Internal Criticism" to "put all its standards under reexamination and to serve as a public protector in its day-to-day operations." [48]
He added:

> The department head ought to be given enough independence in the paper to serve as an ombudsman for the readers, armed with authority to get something done about valid complaints and to propose methods for more effective performance of all the paper's services to the community, particularly the patrol it keeps on the frontiers of thought and action.[49]

Peter B. Clark, publisher of the Detroit *News*, another newsman who has argued the urgent need for improvement in press performance, particularly in the area of news focus, proposed a set of "new power figures" as more appropriate foci than what he described as "old power figures." He urged less emphasis on generals, bureaucrats, entertainers, politicians and more attention to college and university prosessors, career civil servants, television commentators and editors, and newspaper columnists.[50]
Clark also expounded his views of the failures of press in keeping abreast of a developing society:

If I am correct that we have sometimes failed to identify and challenge the men of new power—why have we failed? . . . .

(1) We are all, to some extent, the prisoners of habit. For example, in college we were told who held the power and many of us have never bothered to ask the question again. . . .

(2) We are all, to some extent, lazy. It requires disciplined work precisely to define the concepts of power, diligently to gather empirical data about actual cases, and dispassionately to draw conclusions. Few have done this work. . . .

(3) We are all, to some extent, deceived by the rhetoric of good intentions. As writers, we tend to attach as much importance to words as to deeds. . . . As practicing moralists . . . we attach great importance to good intentions. Good intentions are seldom sufficient conditions for good results and may not always be necessary conditions.

(4) We are all, to some extent, influenced by the national newsgathering and interpreting system . . . the networks and the wires and the biggest city newspapers slowly incline American journalism toward a single point of view. The old journalistic diversity—in which the Emporia *Gazette* could swing some weight—has been replaced by the more monolithic perceptions emanating from NBC, CBS, ABC, the New York *Times*, the Washington *Post*, AP, UPI, some news magazines, and the interests and insights of a talented corps of New York and Washington newsmen. . . .

(5) We are all, to some extent, more likely to criticize strangers than friends. . . .

(6) The younger members of our profession are, to some extent, the captives of a consensus. Many young newsmen share a point of view—an unstated similarity of attitudes—about what is good and what is bad. . . .

What must be challenged is the very existence of any consensus in our profession.[51]

One "old power figure," former Vice-President Spiro Agnew, bitterly challenged exactly what Clark said must be challenged—consensus. On November 13, 1969, speaking to the Republican faithful in Des Moines, Iowa, Agnew accused television network newsmen of "instant analysis" of President Richard Nixon's recent addresses. He said:

> The audience of 70 million Americans . . . was inherited by a small band of network commentators and self-appointed analysts, the majority of whom expressed, in one way or another, their hostility to what he had to say.[52]

Agnew attributed great power to television to shape the opinions of the nation, criticized commentators for having parochial biases, declared that network media distorted the Democratic National Convention riots in 1968, and accused the networks of failing to criticize their own handling of news, particularly in the separation of news and editorial comment. Agnew said:

> We would never trust such power over public opinion in the hands of an elected government—it is time we questioned it in the hands of a small and un-elected elite. The great networks have dominated America's airwaves for decades; the people are entitled to a full accounting of their stewardship.[53]

The press, both print and broadcast, fought back by fleeing to the shelter of the First Amendment. The former vice-president was accused of attempted intimidation of the press particularly through the implicit lines of authority between the administrative branch of government and the Federal Communication Commission. A second-stage reaction from some sectors of the press was that the remarks probably should have been expected because the press and the government are "naturally in conflict" and reciprocal criticism not only should be expected but encouraged.

Agnew's comments occurred during a period in which the press was subjecting itself to searching self-examination particularly in professional and paraprofessional journals. One study of three years (1967 through 1969) of criticism of the press by journalists showed that among the major critical themes was the encouragement of criticism and self-criticism by and of the press. Even so, the critics indicated they resented criticism from government officials and "professional dissenters," but were more willing to accept the critiques of professional critics of the press. Another theme was concern over inaccurate reporting and what was seen as a resultant, growing credibility gap between the reader and viewer-listener on the one hand and the media on the other. The critics thought the gap could be lessened by sound, factual reporting and, when shown an error, a prompt and public correction acknowledging the fact that the press, too, is fallible. A third theme of the criticism of the period indicated the press should get about the business of defining the role of the press. While there was as much disagreement as agreement, many critics thought the press should concern itself with problems of the moment, not of history, and still work to bring the nation together by reducing pluralism and helping to create greater popular consensus on issues of concern to society at large. The press, the critics generally agreed, should continue to "call it as it sees it," but it must call it more precisely and see it with greater depth and integrity. A fourth theme of the self-criticism was that the press should be more concerned with the human condition and critics urged more empathy in writing, reporting and editing. Critics argued for reporting oriented to processes instead of events. They argued against trying to tell a complex story in a simplex form. They disagreed, but at least pursued with vigor the long-standing debates surrounding "truth," "objectivity," and "interpretation" in reporting the news.

The foregoing represents an attempt to establish the

mainstreams of press criticism that began in England in the late 1600s until today in the United States, a period of three hundred years. It is not a comprehensive collection, but it is believed to be representative. Particularly in the contemporary period of criticism, several important developments have been omitted; they will be discussed in subsequent chapters. Among them have been the rise of the professional critic in periodical literature, the development of journals as forums for criticism of the press, the in-house ombudsman-critic, the elusive but often proposed national press council, local press councils, and a series of national reports on violence and civil disorder containing searching criticisms of press performance during crises.

Time has not produced solutions to the perceived failings of the press. In three hundred years the criticism has changed more in expression than in kind, and the basic criticisms have endured and grown through elaboration and repetition. Perhaps the press has maintained through time a stable distance relative to the society it serves or seeks to serve, and perhaps the differences in the performance of the press are ones of cultural epoch and not of quality. Even so, the press seems to have improved and changed far more than have the criticisms of it. What is wrong with the press? The consensus of the critics and their criticisms may be put into three categories divided by function: the press as a vehicle for journalism (reporting, editing, and writing); the press as a social institution; and finally, the press as an economic enterprise.

In the first category, that of journalism, the press has been criticized for inaccuracy, coloring the news in seeking sensation, reductionism, triviality, lack of coherence on a day-to-day basis, superficiality, not taking itself seriously, for invading privacy, for being bound to worn-out criteria (blood, sex, money) for what makes news, and for a lack of editorial leadership.

As a social institution, the press has been indicted for its emphasis on entertainment, for catering to the mob, for catering to the middle class, for being unresponsive to the needs of society, for being conformist and unnecessarily conservative, for limiting the society's access to the media, for lowering popular taste, for being standardized and monolithic, for failing to admit error, for being timid, and for not instituting systems for self-correction.

As an economic enterprise, the press has been criticized for permitting the profit motive priority over serving society's needs, for venality and timidity when faced with opposition from advertisers or powerful economic interests, for accepting false and misleading advertising, for ruthlessness, and for hypocrisy in the sense that advertising content frequently falls short of the professed standards for journalism.

3 THE ANATOMY
OF PRESS CRITICISM:
CONDUCT AND NATURE

"Every newspaperman is a critic of the press,"[1] wrote
A. J. Liebling, but perhaps no one has achieved his
brilliance at it. "Joe" Liebling took over "The
Wayward Press" column in the *New Yorker* in 1945, a
column introduced by Robert Benchley in 1927.
Liebling reigned as the nation's most prominent
professional critic of the press until his death in 1963.
It was not a crowded field, and for at least part of
that period Liebling was most of it.

His criticism was more parochial than it might
have been, concentrating on New York newspapers,
but he was read nationwide and what he wrote was
memorable as much for style as for content. He was a
pithy, pungent writer, sometimes as acerbic as
H. L. Mencken. He carried an ongoing battle against

publishers, wrote little about editors, and was an ombudsman for reporters. His egalitarianism led him to attack newspaper columnists and interpretive analysts. He once wrote:

> There are three kinds of writers of news in our generation. In inverse order of worldly consideration, they are: (1) the reporter, who writes what he sees; (2) the interpretive reporter, who writes what he sees and what he construes to be its meaning; (3) the expert, who writes what he construes to be the meaning of what he hasn't seen.[2]

Yet, about editors, and other newspaper executives, Liebling could say:

> . . . there are in every newspaper office the congenital, aboriginal, intramurals. They are to be distinguished from the frustrates because they have never even wanted to see the world outside. They come to newspapers like monks to cloisters or worms to apples. They are the dedicated. All of them are fated to be editors except the ones that get killed off by the lunches they eat at their desks until even the most drastic purgatives lose all effect upon them. The survivors of gastric disorders rise to minor executive jobs and then major ones, and the reign of these non-writers makes our newspapers read like the food in the New York *Times* cafeteria tastes.[3]

Liebling, who had worked for the New York *World* and later for the *World-Telegram*, once wrote about his purpose as critic of the press, and declared, "I would like to stimulate some criticism among newspapers by newspapers rather than by ink-stained wretches on magazines." [4] While he lived to see great advances in criticism of the press, he apparently entertained no notions about the impact of his own criticisms in changing the press. Midway in his career as critic he wrote, ". . . the longer I criticized the press, the more it disimproved. . . ." [5]

If there was a mantle of professional press critic, it was assumed by Ben Bagdikian, a former Rhode Island newsman and freelance writer who contributed frequently to the *Columbia Journalism Review*, spent a year at the Rand Corporation, and produced *The Information Machines*, a book assessing and predicting revolutionary changes in mass media technology.

Bagdikian's thoughtful critiques of press performance led to his appointment as national editor of the Washington *Post* following his tenure at Rand. In 1967, in a review critical of the *Post*, he suggested five qualities of greatness in an article, "What Makes a Newspaper Nearly Great?" [6] He urged: (1) authority (precise, thorough, balanced reporting), (2) comprehensiveness (all the important developments), (3) art (evidence of style, insight, intelligence), (4) professionalism (basic facts, clear and unpoisoned), and (5) a sense of priority in the news (display and order of stories).

Bagdikian later was appointed ombudsman of the *Post*, succeeding Richard Harwood, the *Post*'s first in-house critic. As did Harwood, Bagdikian handled reader complaints, wrote editorial-page analyses of the *Post*'s foibles, and offered in-house memoranda critical of the *Post*'s performance to Benjamin C. Bradlee, executive editor. Harwood's tenure ended after a year in the fall of 1971; Bagdikian's ended in the fall of 1972.

Bagdikian's tenure as ombudsman ended in a disagreement with other members of management on the role and function of the in-house ombudsman. Bagdikian found that handling reader complaints interfered with the function of general critic. He reported other problems, too, and filed a recommended prescription for the ombudsman position upon his resignation:

1. That the *Post*'s press critic be hired for a short-term, nonrenewable contract.

2. That the critic not be burdened with handling reader complaints.

3. That the critic work outside the newsroom so as to avoid the appearance of undercutting operating editors.

4. That assessments of the work of staff members be shown to those involved, with a right of reply offered.

5. That the critic have space guaranteed in the paper, so as to avoid the charge that the paper prints only what it agrees with.

6. That the critic be a person whose standards are in fundamental agreement with the newspaper's traditions.[7]

Bagdikian was succeeded as ombudsman by Robert C. Maynard, a former Nieman Fellow at Harvard University, who was appointed for an eighteen-month term.

"The job of the Washington *Post* Ombudsman is to monitor the performance of the newspaper in the pursuit of its goals," Bradlee wrote in announcing Maynard's appointment to his staff. He continued, "These goals are to be as truthful, fair, complete, clear and relevant as humanly possible and to be so with courage, energy and enterprise."[8]

If press criticism languished during World War II, it was nascent during the last half of the 1940s and the 1950s. The (Hutchins) Commission on a Free and Responsible Press had called for a national press council in 1947, about the time a national press council first was established in England. While these were less than the shots heard around the world, they served nevertheless as distant early warnings of the paroxysm of criticism that was to come during the 1960s and 1970s in six distinct forms:

—the resurgence of journalist-critic in book and journal
—the appearance of more than a dozen journals for press criticism
—the establishment of local press councils
—the establishment of in-house ombudsmen
—the reports of presidential and other commissions
—the establishment of a national press council

Liebling was not and Bagdikian is not the only prominent critic of the press. In his biography of Liebling, Professor Edmund Midura observed:

> Since Liebling's death Ben Bagdikian has emerged as the leading individual critic of the press, although others—among them Carl Lindstrom, Herbert Brucker, and Harry Ashmore—have published books in the same area. There have even been occasional efforts from the direction of the broadcast media, the most notable being "CBS Views the Press," conducted by Don Hollenbeck in the late Forties, and "WCBS-TV (New York) Views the Press," conducted by Charles Collingwood in the late 1950s and early 1960s.[9]

Expanding upon Midura's summation, there have been other important critics of the press. Some of them have impacted professional practice, most of them have influenced journalism education, and some of them have been read by the public at large.

Harry S. Ashmore, associated with the Center for the Study of Democratic Institutions in California, won a Pulitzer Prize when he was editor of the Arkansas *Gazette* and was a Nieman Fellow. He has argued for a national press council modeled after that proposed by the (Hutchins) Commission for a Free and Responsible Press. He also has argued that newspapers will be unable to compete with television journalism unless they can encourage intellectual readership and become centers of learning. He views the role of the newspaper as explaining, clarifying and expanding television news coverage.

Norman E. Isaacs, then editor of the Louisville *Courier Journal*, and president of the American Society of Newspaper Editors, unsuccessfully sought an ASNE national grievance committee to give the public a voice and channel for criticism of unfair or unethical practices. He wrote that such a committee would help the press retain credibility.

Ralph McGill, the late publisher of the Atlanta *Constitution,* was an advocate of interpretive reporting. He argued that the cult of objectivity sometimes prevented truthful reporting; he urged the press to reexamine "old style" techniques in order to keep abreast of social changes resulting from technology, and he opined that the nation's press has failed to recognize what was happening and, thus, to give meaning to it through structured interpretation.

Nat Hentoff, of the New York *Village Voice* and an occasional contributor to *Saturday Review,* has urged greater public access to newspapers. He has recommended expanded letters-to-the-editor sections, expanded editorial and column sections, the appointment of resident ombudsmen for readers, and the use of press councils.

Carl E. Lindstrom wrote *The Fading American Newspapers* in 1960. He proposed that the press must not merely reflect life, but must project it to the common man. He wrote that editors and publishers have a pathological fear of criticism. He also maintained that the press takes for granted its function as critic, but mortgages its right to criticize others when it fails to criticize itself vigorously. He predicted that newspapers will be more valuable to society when they become less abbreviated and adopt the "whole story" formula that has made weekly news magazines successful.

Herbert Brucker, a frequent contributor to magazines on the press, unlike McGill, has argued that newspapers must "regrasp old-school objectivity." He has observed that objectivity should be the ruling influence in journalism, that newspapers should not become propaganda vehicles for activist reporters, and that in a society filled with extremists, the highest goal a newsman can try for is that of impartiality.

William L. Rivers, a one-time Washington newsman and later a professor of journalism at Stanford University, has been active in the establishment of local press councils and has urged establishment of a national press council, something on the order of the British Press Council, but made up entirely of members of the media. He has observed that as issues become less simple, the reporter must also be interpreter and analyst of what he witnesses.

I. F. Stone, retired self-educated editor-publisher of *I. F. Stone's Weekly*, has been a declaimer of "big-shot" journalists. He has argued for "gutsy" journalism, journalism that provokes the readers to anger. He found most journalistic practice permitting government and big business to do as they please unchecked and unchallenged by the press.

J. Russell Wiggins, retired executive editor of the Washington *Post*, has criticized the press for its complacency in the face of government secrecy, for emphasizing trivia and entertainment on pages that could be devoted to news of substance, and for overreliance on syndicated materials. He has argued that the seemingly perverse image of the press as tellers only of bad news is a reflection of society in general and, besides, people are more interested in bad news than they are in good news.

Jules Witcover, formerly of the Los Angeles *Times* and more recently of the Washington *Post*, has maintained that the information explosion means the press must abandon outdated "beat" coverage and allow newsmen more time to develop stories fully. He has contended that part of the press credibility decline may be the increasing trend toward interpretive and analytical reporting and comment which has blurred the lines between reporting and analysis. He wrote that public acceptance of police attacks upon newsmen during the riots that attended the Democratic National Convention in Chicago in 1968 indicate there is a widening credibility gap between the American public and journalism.

Tom Wolfe, a former New York newsman turned novelist, is one of the few pioneers in what has popularly been called the "new journalism." Wolfe has said that he turned from newspaper reporting because it lacked substance, and was too bland and neutral. He has argued that "understatement" has fallen over conventional journalism as an absolute pall, but that innovative "new journalists" such as Gay Talese, Jimmy Breslin, and Nicholas von Hoffman have made penetrating contributions toward giving the reader a more total picture of events.

The new ascension of writing press critics would have been impossible without vehicles for their efforts. The spate of local journals for criticism of the press began in 1968 with the establishment of the *Chicago Journalism Review*. In the following four years, it was followed into print by more than a dozen others, only one of which, [*More*], attempts a national audience and seeks profit. Most are aimed at and consumed by journalists and others closely associated with the print and broadcast press, and mostly in small geographical areas. The sudden proliferation of journals about journalism corresponds with the growth of special interest publications in all fields, including recreation, special interests, and professional.

The new wave, however, had several magisterial predecessors in the *Bulletin* of the American Society of Newspaper Editors, *Nieman Reports, Grassroots Editor*, and the *Columbia Journalism Review*.

The *Bulletin* of the American Society of Newspaper Editors began with the founding of its parent organization in 1922 as a mimeographed sheet. It wasn't printed until early in the 1930s. Its criticisms of the press were sparse and apparently based on what the editors felt were "as needed" occurrences. The *Bulletin* content began to reflect a growing interest in press criticism in the early 1960s; by the end of that decade much of its content was devoted to criticizing the press and the critics frequently have been editors and others prominent in journalistic circles.

Nieman Reports was founded in 1947 at Harvard

University as adjunct to the Nieman Fellowship program. One of its founders, Louis M. Lyons, the long-time Nieman Foundation curator, wrote in 1968 of the publication's birth:

> Responsibility of the press is a concept introduced by the Hutchins Commission, or at least given currency by that report. The publishers who scoffed at it as an academic notion in 1947 have long since adopted it into their vocabulary. I am sure many of them think they invented it. It became at once the basic theme of *Nieman Reports* and has threaded through the reviews, critiques, and articles (since). . . . *Nieman Reports* took its tone, found its philosophy, and built its course on the responsibility of the press.[10]

Somewhat as has the *Bulletin, Nieman Reports* has been dominated by Nieman Fellows and former fellows, by editors and, to a lesser extent, by journalism professors and by distinguished reporters. This was to be true of *Grassroots Editor*, the principal contributors of which have been editors of outstanding weekly papers, and of *Columbia Journalism Review*, a prestigious publication affiliated with the Graduate School of Journalism at Columbia University.

Grassroots Editor was founded in 1960 by H. R. Long, of Southern Illinois University, to be the publication of the International Conference of Weekly Newspaper Editors. While its format was modeled after *Nieman Reports*, its content was not. The publication sought to emphasize its international aspect, and directed its domestic energies at weekly editors who were serious about the role of other-than-metropolitan journalism and who were successful. While its purpose was not to criticize the press, many of its contributions have proved themselves critics.

Hard on its heels, *Columbia Journalism Review* was founded at Columbia University. The inside cover of its first edition proclaimed its purpose, "to assess the performance of journalism in all its forms, to call attention to its

shortcomings and its strengths, and to help define
—or redefine—standards of honest, responsible
service."

As in the instance of its predecessors, *CJR* was not a
major financial success, although it sought subscribers
throughout the nation as had the other three publications,
and perhaps more aggressively. In 1967 *CJR* received a
$195,000 grant from the Ford Foundation, "to be used to
support and strengthen the Review and to help it develop
resources for long-term financial support."

CJR instantly became the most handsome publication in
its field. It attracted contributors of established stature and
others who acquired stature by contributing. For most of the
1960s, though, the public could read about the press regularly
in weekly news magazines, in *Saturday Review*'s monthly
communication section, and in occasional articles in other
magazines of general interest and national circulation. For
the most part, only persons directly associated with the press
read the *Bulletin*, *Nieman Reports*, *Grassroots Editor*, and
CJR.

As Professor Midura observed:

> . . . our supposedly least-criticized institution [the
> press] has certainly not gone uncriticized, no matter
> how ungracious its reaction has occasionally been . . .
> criticism of press performance has come from within the
> press itself, although it has been inwardly directed . . .
> the general public has had little part in their dialogue
> and has rarely been apprised of it.[11]

The dam was broken in 1968 with the founding of the
Chicago Journalism Review following the Democratic
National Convention in that city. Several years later, the
Chicago review was characterized by *Time* as the best of the
newcomers, but unlike the *Columbia Journalism Review*
because it was, with other new journalism journals, "blunt,

angry, and gossipy in their exposure of faults, real or imagined. Most are financially fragile, physically unprepossessing, and dependent on volunteered talent." [12] The *Chicago Journalism Review*, unlike its predecessors, was founded in a spirit of protest, particularly over the belief that the Chicago press was enjoying a too-cozy relationship with Mayor Richard Daley and his powerful political machine. One founder-editor, Ron Dorfman, later assisted in the establishment of a number of other journalism reviews. The spirit of protest underlying the new journals turned to a spirit of crusade against what was seen as a stodgy, establishment press, too placid to encourage wave making, and too timid to turn over rocks in order to find worms. H. L. Mencken, a distinguished journalist, scholar, editor, and author, once characterized the American people as "timorous, sniveling, poltroonish and ignominious," and this is what the new journals of criticism were saying of a large portion of the American press, publishers, and top editors.

In 1972, when the American Newspaper Publishers Association held its annual convention in the Waldorf-Astoria in New York, [*More*] sponsored the A. J. Liebling Counter-Convention nearby, but in a less splendid atmosphere. [*More*], at the time of its ninth issue, was able to observe that its subscription list already was over 5,000 and boast that newsstand sales across the nation had grown to 3,000. The counter-convention attracted more than a handful of distinguished American journalists, some of the self-declared avant-garde of the press, journalism professors, and a host of curious or the disenchanted newsmen and women from around the nation. The assemblage used Liebling's antipathy for publishers to underscore and symbolize its own dissatisfaction with American journalism.

Between 1968 and 1973, journalism reviews were established in Baltimore (*Buncombe*), Denver (*The Unsatisfied Man*), Holyoke (*Thorn*), Honolulu (*Hawaii*

Journalism Review), Houston (*Houston Journalism Review*),
Long Beach (*Southern California Journalism Review*), New
York City ([*More*]), Philadelphia (*Philadelphia Journalism
Review*), Portland (*Oregon Journalism Review*), Providence
(*Journalists Newsletter*), San Francisco (*San Francisco Bay
Area Journalism Review*), St. Louis (*St. Louis Journalism
Review*), and St. Paul (*Twin Cities Journalism Review*).

Their introduction sometimes was met with suspicion
and often with outright hostility by management of the
media units most directly concerned with being victims of
the journals' often acrid criticisms. The *Oregon Journalism
Review* died after five months amid allegations of pressure
and threats from the management of the Portland *Oregonian*.
Threats of dismissal, demotion, changes to less desirable
assignments, and, simply, falling from favor, reportedly
attended the establishment of most of the reviews, and in
some instances, the threats became reality. Most reviews
required bylines for contributions, a policy that increased the
vulnerability of the contributor while adding to the
credibility of the publications.

"Contributors are mostly junior staffers from local
papers; criticism has often been narrow and carping, more
concerned with working conditions than the paper's
performance; advocacy sometimes is so one-sided as to seem
irresponsible." [13]

Buncombe failed in 1973, the year after its founding,
because of a paucity of contributors. While it was funded
better than some reviews, no one wrote for it.

Many editors argue that they approve of the idea of
journalism reviews in the spirit of criticism and in the airing
of genuine problems, to what they see as implicit disloyalty,
invective, pettiness, tale-telling, whining, and the mere airing
of personal grievances. At the same time, many contributors
write about what they see as news suppression and
manipulation, sexism, arrogation, racism, and sacred-cow

policies. According to Bagdikian, the journalism reviews with growth and maturity may "strengthen those voices in the wilderness who really care about the profession."[14]

Another similar publication produced its first production issue in 1972 after a promotion issue had headlined, "Oh, no, not another journalism magazine." *Overset*, published in San Diego by Robert Juran, set out to discuss and analyze what it saw as good and bad newspaper journalism with: "We hold no brief for anything except better newspapers. That will be our message and our mission." It ended publication the following year.

Another important development in press criticism has been the emergence of the local press council. Originally, the local press council was thought of as an alternative to a national press council, but it was to become a desirable alternative to many persons who were interested in improving the performance of the press on the one hand, and, on the other, helping consumers realize that the press indeed had improved or was willing to. Proponents of the local or regional press council contend that the local council is able to put a newspaper or broadcast station in direct touch with its immediate consumers, something a national press council would have difficulty accomplishing in a nation as large as this, with thousands of print and broadcast media units.

The first local press council was established in 1946 by Houstoun Waring, publisher of the Littleton (Colo.) *Independent*. It lasted six years, with eight newspaper editors meeting regularly with eight critics, each representing a different segment of the greater community. Called the Colorado Editorial Advisory Board, it was reestablished in 1967 as a permanent press council for the *Independent* and the Arapahoe *Herald*, weeklies under the same ownership.

Another press council was established in 1950 in Santa Rosa, California, by William Townes, publisher of the *Press-Democrat*. Townes selected what essentially was a "blue-ribbon" committee to offer suggestions and criticisms about what the paper ought to do for the community. It lasted only a year, until Townes left, but *Editor & Publisher* observed at the time:

> On the practical side, this particular newspaper reports that council meetings revealed several important stories that had not been covered. And council members felt free to visit the newspaper offices thereafter, something many of them might not have thought about previously.[15]

In 1963, Harry Bingham, president and editor of the Louisville *Courier-Journal* and *Times*, publicly proposed the creation of a local press council to serve as a forum for his own papers and the consumers of them. Nothing happened on the council proposal, and one account attributed this to citizen apathy, but Bingham did establish a full-time ombudsman to respond to reader complaints about his papers.

In 1967, when Ben Bagdikian became president of the Mellett Fund for a Free and Responsible Press, a program began that was to result in six press councils, four of them limited to newspapers and two of them including broadcasters as well as publishers. The Mellett Fund had a small endowment—$40,000—but, in collaboration with university journalism professors and the Association for Education in Journalism, moved to establish local councils that would serve as vehicles for better communication and understanding between the press and its consumers. Professor William Rivers of Stanford University and Professor William B. Blankenburg, since of the University of Wisconsin but then with Rivers at Stanford, worked together in establishing and working with nine-member councils in Redwood City, California, and in Bend, Oregon. Professor Kenneth Starck, then of Southern Illinois University, established and worked with the press councils in Sparta and Cairo, Illinois. Dr. Earl Reeves, then of the University of Missouri–St. Louis, performed similar functions for the St. Louis Press Council. Another press council, in Seattle, survived after the St. Louis council atrophied because of better success in involving its black community in council affairs.

The Mellett-sponsored councils had differing experiences, apparently none of them dysfunctional. In sum, publishers were able to report that the public had learned something about the problems of publishing and broadcasting, particularly the former, and that media executives discovered to their benefit something of the needs of their respective communities. They discovered that press performance and public expectations were not always in accord in an atmosphere that made it possible for mutual education and adjustment. Most of the Mellett-sponsored councils ran for a nine-month period, but several continued on because the endeavor seemed worthwhile.

In 1973, Howard W. Hays, Jr., editor and co-publisher of the Riverside (Calif.) *Press* and *Daily Enterprise*, invited prominent persons in his community to join an eleven-member Riverside Press Council. Hays established a paid consultant, Roger Tatarian, retired *United Press International* editor, and committed the paper to publishing in full the council's reports. Hays set up the council with the notion that it would be a one-year experiment. The council's objectives, he announced, would be to:

Give the newspapers the benefit of its suggestions and criticism.

Give council members an opportunity to discuss the content of the newspapers with those responsible for it, promote public accountability of the press, and help maintain high standards of journalism.

Give the readers of the newspapers another channel

for their complaints about, or observations on, the newspapers.

Provide the readers of the newspapers and the community generally with periodic and independent reports on the performance of the newspapers.[16]

Two state press councils have been established in the United States, one in Minnesota (1971) and the other in Honolulu, Hawaii (1969). The Honolulu press council has the effect of a state press council because all of Hawaii's statewide media operate out of Honolulu. In Canada, similarly, provincial press councils have been established in Alberta, supported by five daily newspapers, and in Ontario, sponsored by eight newspapers.

The Minnesota Press Council was formed by the Minnesota Newspaper Association with eighteen members, half of them representing the press and the other half representing the public. Minnesota Supreme Court Associate Justice C. Donald Peterson was named the first chairman of the council, which adopted operating rules along the lines of the British Press Council.

In general, press councils have been devised with common features:

1. They are private, disassociated from government at any level.
2. They operate as an intermediary between the press and the public, and in the process educate both.
3. They are composed of representatives, usually executives, of the press and the public, usually prominent persons in the community.
4. They have no coercive or official powers.
5. They draw up rules to govern their operations.
6. They often concern themselves with questions of commission and omission in news coverage, ethics, fair play and balance in news and editorial content.

The fourth distinct form of press criticism that was to emerge during the 1960s and 1970s is the already mentioned in-house ombudsman. The word "ombudsman" is considerably newer to American journalism than the function implied by it. In 1913, Ralph Pulitzer established the Bureau of Accuracy and Fair Play of the New York *World* to investigate reader complaints and to order corrections when appropriate. In 1924, the Detroit *News* employed an "editorial secretary" to perform a similar function.[17]

The role of the ombudsman of the Washington *Post* already has been outlined here, but the first "modern" ombudsman predated the *Post*'s by several years. John Herchenroeder, city editor of the Louisville *Courier-Journal* for more than twenty years, was appointed ombudsman in 1967 for the *Courier-Journal* and the *Times*.

In 1972, *Editor & Publisher* reported:

> Some of the more than 6,000 calls and letters have convinced Herch that there is an increased awareness of readers as to how news is gathered, written and played; a new sensitivity which causes them to voice their opinions based on their own news judgments.[18]

The Louisville papers also established two features for corrections, "We Were Wrong" in one, and "Beg Your Pardon" in the other. In addition, on the back page of each paper's first section appears daily an invitation that questions or complaints be directed to Herchenroeder, with his telephone number.

Elsewhere during the same period, the Minneapolis *Star* and *Tribune* established an ombudsman function with its "Readers Referee" and the "Bureau of Accuracy and Fair Play" to deal with reader complaints and comments. Another newspaper, the St. Petersburg *Times*, has commissioned a staff member to serve an ombudsman function to investigate and respond to readers who voice complaints.

An ANPA News Research Center Study, "A Survey of U.S. Daily Newspaper Accountability Systems," reported in 1973 that other papers with an ombudsman or similar person include: the Wilmington (Del.) *News* and *Journal*, the Delta (Miss.) *Democrat-Times*, the Grand Rapids *Press*, the Dayton *Journal Herald*, the Salt Lake *Tribune*, the New Castle (Pa.) *News*, the Omaha *World-Herald*, the Milwaukee *Journal*, the Easton (Pa.) *Express*, the Rockford (Ill.) *Star and Register*, the Lafayette (Ind.) *Journal and Courier*, and the Utica (N.Y.) *Observer-Dispatch*.[19]

The same study, which included two hundred newspapers, found that more than half of the studied newspapers have developed a system to be accountable to readers, the most common one being the mailing out of accuracy forms to persons mentioned in stories. It found, moreover, that some papers print accuracy forms routinely so they are available to all readers. Many newspapers, including the New York *Times*, print corrections under a standing headline.

The study also uncovered considerable opposition from responding editors to ombudsmen, press councils, and other special accountability systems. It indicated that many editors felt that accountability was a by-product of good journalistic practice, and that care and thoroughness with a willingness to print corrections were adequate measures for accountability to the public. Other editors, the study found, were pleased with the special accountability systems their newspapers had developed. A number of the papers, according to the survey, had developed more than one accountability system.

Another major course of criticism of the press during the 1960s came in the form of quasi-official commission reports, some of them instituted at the order of President Lyndon B. Johnson. Unanimously, they reported what many members of the press least wanted to hear, that the press was part of the nation's problems, not merely a detached observer and chronicler of them.

The first presidential commission of that period was the Warren Commission on the Assassination of President John F. Kennedy. Headed by U.S. Supreme Court Chief Justice Earl Warren, the report of the commission emphasized what it saw as the abridgement of the rights of the accused assassin, Lee Harvey Oswald. Oswald was fatally shot by a Dallas nightclub owner, Jack Ruby, who had joined a crowd of newsmen eager to question Oswald. The Warren Commission found the press guilty on several counts: for failing to observe the rights of the accused, for failing to police its own membership and maintain order during the few hours that Oswald survived in the Dallas Police Station following his arrest, for reporting details police believed were associated with the crime but which led to erroneous conclusions and conflicting accounts, for transmitting misinformation to the public, for transmitting prejudicial (to a trial) information, for not having preestablished ethical standards of conduct for newsmen.

Massive racial conflict in Los Angeles during 1965, the so-called Watts Riot, led to the establishment by California Governor Edmund G. Brown of the Governor's Commission on the Los Angeles Riots, headed by John A. McCone. The commission's report was gently pointed about press conduct during the riots and even about the reporting of racial affairs before the rioting. The McCone report suggested that the highest traditions of a free press involve responsibility as well as drama, and that the press had overemphasized inflammatory incidents at the expense of constructive developments, particularly in the early hours of the riot. The report urged that the press adopt voluntary guidelines for the responsible reporting of such disasters.

Three years later, after more summers of civil strife in a half-dozen major cities, the Kerner Commission filed the report of the National Advisory Commission on Civil

Disorders. The Kerner Commission (after former Illinois Governor Otto Kerner) reported that while the press attempted balanced, factual accounts of disorders, the overall effect of the reportage was exaggeration of both mood and event. The report argued that the media too often failed to achieve a sufficient level of sophisticated, skeptical, careful news judgment to portray situations accurately, particularly in the reporting of events that, while true in isolation, were not representative of the situations overall. It also suggested that the press was white-dominated to the extent that its daily coverage was distorted by Caucasian bias, however unintended. It also pointed out that the press had failed to establish suitable rapport or guidelines with civil authorities, particularly the police, to prevent distortion during times of major civil disorder.

The National Commission on Causes and Prevention of Violence released its report following the riots in Chicago in 1968 during which, it found, forty-nine newsmen were hit, sprayed with a chemical similar to tear gas, or arrested, apparently without reason by Chicago police. The Commission's criticism of the press was indirect, and the least critical of all the major commission reports. It cautioned against inexpert use of cameras, bright lights and microphones because exhibitionists might be stirred to action. It urged that only seasoned reporters be sent to the scenes of disasters or major conflicts. It admonished that reporters and technicians should be governed by rules of good taste and common sense, and that competition be subordinated to the cause of public safety. However, it also recognized that Chicago police, some segments of the public, and some public officials blamed the mass media for at least some complicity in causing the violence that flared during the Democratic National Convention.

With the growing movement for a national press council, these have become the principal forms of contemporary press criticism: the resurgent journalist-critic;

the journal, particularly the local journal, for criticism of the press; the establishment of local press councils, by individual publishers and under the auspices of the Mellett Fund; the establishment of in-house ombudsmen, on only a few newspapers, to respond to reader complaints; and the reports of presidential and other commissions. In sum, they represent a significant force in press criticism hitherto not experienced in American journalism. An additional dimension of the critical force of these developments is that each has been widely discussed in trade journals and other literature associated with journalism, as well as in the print and broadcast media themselves. Among the former are *Journal of Broadcasting, Editor & Publisher*, the *Quill, TV Guide*, the Associated Press Managing Editors *Redbook, Masthead*, and Radio-Television News Directors *Journal*.

Another source of criticism of the press has been that of the legal establishment, from the Supreme Court to law professors to committees of the American Bar Association.

A professor of law at Georgetown University, Jerome A. Barron, proposed in 1967 that the First Amendment to the Constitution required a new interpretation, and that every citizen deserved a right of access to the press. His argument rested on increasing media monopoly, chain ownership, and centralization of press power, and that freedom of the press thus was enjoyed by only a few publishers. He also argued that the easy access of every citizen to a mimeograph machine or similar inexpensive duplicating process was inadequate because, independent of necessary limitations upon circulation, they lack efficacy. Professor Barron's arguments exceed the Federal Communication Commission's "right of reply" or the "right of equal time"; they propose that any citizen has the right to initiate discussion on any question in the mass media, and that space or time be guaranteed. He continued that only in this way can the mass media become a true marketplace for ideas.

Alternatives to Barron's widely discussed proposal have included antitrust legislation as well as legislation to require the media to accept all lawful advertisements. Beyond that, the access proposal has received short shrift from journalists. Some have argued that it is impractical, that to guarantee space in a newspaper to everyone who wanted it would leave no room (or time) for news. Moreover, journalists have argued that journalists alone are qualified to determine what goes into the newspaper, not courts, legislatures, or private persons. Editors have responded, if a compellingly good idea somehow doesn't make the space allotted to letters to the editor, the mimeograph should be good enough to get it off the ground. Finally, there is a pervasive feeling among those protected by the First Amendment that the best thing to do is not to tinker with it.

Few developments during the 1960s raised as much furor among the newsgathering fraternity as the Reardon* Report for the American Bar Association recommending new guidelines restricting access of the press to information about suspects prior to trial. To many journalists, the report was a blatant attempt to muzzle the press and protect the judicial process from journalistic scrutiny. The recommendations, which came to have the force of law, did not deal directly with the press. They restricted officers of the law and the courts from making public information concerning the prior police record, confessions, or materials that would not be presented at trial. The result was that oft-frequented wells of information simply dried up. One response was that of Robert C. Norton, the ASNE president, and J. Edward Murray, then chairman of the society's Press-Bar and Freedom of Information Center Committee. They issued a rebuttal statement citing a converse report, that of the Medina Committee Report on Fair Trial and Free Press.[20] They said:

* After Paul Reardon, chief justice, Massachusetts Supreme Court.

We think the Medina Committee is eminently correct in:

1. Saying the Bill of Rights and the Constitution prohibit statutory and court control over the press and police in release and publication of pretrial information and

2. Condemning as unconstitutional the wave of judicial strictures that has issued across the nation in recent weeks and

3. Rejecting extension of contempt powers by the courts over the press.[21]

The considerable backlash of the press notwithstanding, more than thirty states later were to see the formation of "free press-fair trial" committees, usually the result of cooperation between state press associations and state bar associations.

Another issue involving pretrial publicity went to the Supreme Court in 1966, and involved a decision laden with tacit criticism of the press. Dr. Samuel Sheppard was convicted of murdering his wife in Ohio in 1954 after an investigation and trial accompanied by widespread and intense news coverage. Unsuccessfully, Sheppard tried several appeal routes. Finally, the Supreme Court reversed Sheppard's conviction on the basis that the trial judge had failed to protect him from massive, pervasive and prejudicial publicity. It was to become the case most often cited by defenders of the Reardon Report.

The largesse of the critic in his criticism has been cornucopian. Abjurers in the press have been many and resolute. One midwestern editor found professional press critics sounding "like the celibate clergy lecturing on birth control." Another editor complained about catching "hell from all sides" and said, "Some retired editors, professors of journalism and the Bagdikian types who write for money will peck away as always." One publisher who agreed to participate in the Mellett Fund press councils reported receiving letters from an executive of the *Wall Street Journal* asking, "Why are you giving up your press freedom?"[22]

The reformation in press criticism often has been reluctant. It frequently has been met with skepticism, distrust and even disavowal. Yet, as the watchdogs of society discovered themselves watched more closely, more systematically and more publicly than ever before, growing numbers of journalists and citizens added their energies to the avalanche of criticism aimed at improving the press in an era of social disaffection.

4 THE NATIONAL PRESS COUNCIL: FROM FDR TO XANADU?

In the darkness of the economic depression that began in 1928, President Franklin D. Roosevelt took unprecedented steps to restore economic stability during his first term of office. Part of his "New Deal" legislation was the National Industrial Recovery Act, passed by Congress in 1933, and part of the act contained a provision for a Newspaper Industrial Board. The principal function of the NIB was to investigate complaints of violation of the NIRA, which set a minimum wage of $11 a week for full-time newspaper employees on small papers, established a week as five days or forty hours, and limited the conditions under which children could be employed.

The American Newspaper Publishers Association

established a committee of twenty-five publishers to represent it in helping to prepare what was to become the Daily Newspaper Code. But the editorial furies of much of the nation's press were unleashed against Roosevelt, against NIRA administrators, and against supporters of either. Many publishers saw the act and the code as an attempt to license newspapers and thus curtail freedom of the press; the government took the position that only industry units cooperating with the NIRA could display its emblem, the Blue Eagle. Other newspapers saw the code simply as part of the new labor legislation affecting every sector of domestic industry. As the battle raged on, publishers insisted upon—and received—an article in the code that confirmed the constitutional guarantees of freedom of the press. Moreover, the code contained no fair business practice clause, a provision common in other industrial codes. The American Society of Newspaper Editors sided with the ANPA in its efforts to shape the code in its favor and concluded eventually that the successes constituted "a memorable battle and glorious victory." [1] Meanwhile, the Roosevelt administration continued to deny any plans to license newspapers and eschewed accusations of any attempt to suppress freedom of the press.

Roosevelt said at the time he signed the code into law in 1934:

> The freedom guaranteed by the Constitution is freedom of expression and that will be scrupulously respected—but it is not freedom to work children or to do business in a fire trap or violate the laws against obscenity, libel and lewdness. [2]

One of the by-products of the Newspaper Code was the establishment of the American Newspaper Guild, the first trade organization of editorial employees. Directly, though, little was accomplished by the Code Authority Board in its brief tenure. In 1935, the Supreme Court found that the entire NIRA was unconstitutional, a ruling that included the newspaper provisions. Then died the first national council on the press, albeit a council quite different than those to be suggested in ensuing years.

During the editorial debates attending the code, William Randolph Hearst had thundered from his editorial podium:

> . . . what the publishers throughout the country are concerned about and have been fighting for is the preservation of their constitutional rights of press freedom. . . . The publishers of the country WILL NOT RELINQUISH ANY FRACTION OF THAT GUARANTEED CONSTITUTIONAL RIGHT FOR A FREE PRESS, and they have made that fight more in the interest of the public than in their own interest.[3]

Thirteen years later, the nation's press was to respond similarly to the (Hutchins) Commission on a Free and Responsible Press when it called for a national press council to monitor and evaluate the responsibility of the press. The commission recommended "the establishment of a new and independent agency to appraise and report annually upon the performance of the press,"[4] and further proposed that its membership not include representatives of the press or of the government.

Where the report was not ignored, it was counterattacked by a shocked, derisive press. Harry S. Ashmore, a member of the American Society of Newspaper Editors in 1947, later recalled the reaction of the ASNE to the report. He wrote:

> I . . . saw the august membership huddle rumps together, horns out, in the immemorial manner of, say, the National Association of Manufacturers faced by a threat of regulated prices.[5]

The counterattack—and the press generally felt it had been, indeed, attacked—was pervasive. Frank L. Hughes, for example, a Chicago *Tribune* newsman, took a one-year leave of absence to do research for a book-length rebuttal to the report. His project reached fruition in 1950 in a volume entitled *Prejudice and the Press.*

Twenty-five years after the Hutchins report was released, the Twentieth Century Fund not only called for a national press council, but announced that it was going to establish one in 1973. In spirit and rationale, the reaction from much of the press bore striking resemblances to the fiery pronouncements of Hearst and others nearly four decades earlier.

The New York *Daily News* scoffed:

We don't care how much the Fund prates about its virtuous intentions. This is a sneak attempt at press regulation, a bid for a role as unofficial news censor. The best way to preserve a free press is to permit it to continue policing its own ethics. . . .[6]

The St. Louis *Globe-Democrat* responded to the national press council proposal with:

The proposed council . . . threatens public censorship of the press in a move that could imperil the press of the country in an arbitrary straitjacket. . . . This council's design could erode freedom of the press and the spoken word by the weight of endowed propaganda.[7]

The Detroit *News* asked:

Who will keep it [the council] from playing the role of censor and holding a club over writers and editors as they seek to exercise their rights under the First Amendment?[8]

Not in an editorial, but in a staff memorandum,
A. M. Rosenthal, managing editor of the New York *Times*,
also saw in the council a threat to freedom of the press,
particularly because a national press council could become
simply an aimplifier for special interest or pressure groups
"skilled in the methods of political propaganda." The *Times*
would not cooperate with the council, according to
Rosenthal.

The press was divided by Roosevelt's code in 1934, and
many papers supported the NIRA, including the newspaper
code. The substantial opposition was led by Hearst papers
and the Chicago *Tribune*. But in 1947 nearly all of the nation's
press opposed the Hutchins proposal for a national council
on the press. In 1973 the press again was divided, and a
minority of newspapers gave at least cautious support for the
national council. But the timing of the announcement was
unfortunate for the Twentieth Century Fund.

First, many members of the press had become newly
sensitive to the barrage of criticism already extant. Second,
the announcement came at a time when many journalists
were reacting to what they felt was a particularly hostile
posturing of the administration of President Richard Nixon.
The administration not only had attacked television
commentators and what it saw as a press dominated by
liberal easterners, it also drafted legislation that would hold
local television stations responsible for the content of
network news broadcasting containing what it described as
"ideological plugola." The administration also had sought to
prevent publication of documents outlining the origins of
the U.S. involvement in the Vietnam conflict, and had grown
increasingly remote and secretive during charges of
clandestine eavesdropping on the Democratic National
Headquarters during the campaign of 1972. Reporters from
the Washington *Post* were ignored at the White House.
Third, the judicial establishment at both federal and state
levels was challenging on a dozen different fronts the

traditional prerogative of journalists to protect with silence the sources of their information. Finally, a poll of the nation's editors only a few months before had indicated that a resounding majority of them were in opposition to a national grievance council first proposed for the ASNE in 1969. The Ethics Committee of ASNE asked 740 members by questionnaire shortly before the Twentieth Century Fund announced its intentions:

—Would the membership favor an ASNE grievance committee to receive complaints alleging unethical newspaper practice and to pass judgment upon them?
—Should ASNE cooperate with grievance machinery established by an organization other than ASNE?
—If not, should individual editors cooperate on their own terms?
—Should ASNE establish as record its endorsement of press councils at state or local levels?

Of 405 editors responding, 89 favored, 306 opposed, and 10 were undecided on the ASNE establishing its own grievance committee.

On the question of ASNE support of grievance machinery by another organization, the vote was 257 negative and 106 affirmative.

The response was favorable for individual editors co-operating with press councils on their own terms, 180 to 99.

On the question of whether the editors would support a press council in their area, the response was negative, 234 to 122.

Even more negative was the response of the editors to the question of whether ASNE should officially favor press councils, 296 to 92.[9] The response led *Editor & Publisher* to comment later:

With that sort of antipathy to the whole idea, it is going to be interesting to see whether the national council proposed by the Twentieth Century Fund will be able to function at all.[10]

The New York-based Twentieth Century Fund had announced it would establish a national press council to monitor press performance and to defend the press against governmental and public attacks and that it would operate more or less as do the British and the Minnesota press councils.

In sum, the Fund proposed that the council would:

—Receive, examine and report on complaints concerning accuracy and fairness of news coverage, as well as study and report on issues involving freedom of the press.

—Establish as its concern the principal national suppliers of news, including wire service, supplemental wire services, weekly news magazines, syndicates, national daily newspapers, and nationwide television networks.

—Establish a grievance committee to meet eight and twelve times a year to screen complaints and, when necessary, engage teams to investigate them.

—Issue findings in reports and press releases.

—Require complainants to waive the right to legal proceedings in court on matters considered in Council proceedings.

—Initiate inquiry into any situation where governmental action threatens freedom of the press.

—Seek funding to establish a minimum budget of $400,000 a year for a minimum of three to six years.[11]

In overview, the proposal established that the fund preferred local or regional councils, and would attempt to serve as a model for them. History thus was reversed; the earlier, local councils were formed, in part, because there was no national press council.

The fund named Robert Traynor,* former chief justice of California's Supreme Court, head of the founding committee

* Traynor resigned in 1974 to take a teaching position at Cambridge University, England. He was succeeded by Stanley H. Field, retired chief judge of the New York Court of Appeals.

and chairman of the council. It also set about raising money for the council, and in February 1973, was able to report commitments totaling $250,000 for each of three years.[12]

By the end of 1973, the council was experiencing difficulties. Its executive director, William B. Arthur, the former editor of *Look* magazine, complained that the council was unknown to a large segment of the public. Simply, the council was not receiving the complaints against major news suppliers it had expected.

Arthur acknowledged that the council had received letters from "professional letter writers" and a number of complaints from the Accuracy in Media organization based in Washington, but he said the complaints were not of a nature upon which the council could act.

He said the council had received complaints alleging nationwide media bias on the abortion issue, alleging one television commentator "leered" when President Nixon's name was mentioned, and alleging one newspaper inaccurately reported a "new" cure for gonorrhea.

The council did undertake a study of "the potential threat to a free press posed by increased demands for access to the media" as a result of a Florida court decision extending a Federal Communication Commission equal time provision to newspaper editorials during political campaigns.

It also set out to study President Nixon's charges that television network coverage of him was "outrageous, vicious and distorted." The council deferred further action on the allegations early in 1974 when it announced it had been unable to secure from the White House documentation or "specific instances" in support of the charges.

Arthur indicated that the council intended to play a useful role as a buffer between the public and the media and the government.

The negativism of part of the press toward the council and the lack of public response to the council served to support the major arguments that had developed against the national press council:

—One could do no good and improve nothing because there wasn't a popular or a professional market for one.

—A national news council could serve as a vehicle for official government influence or even a takeover of the nation's press.

—The council would suggest elitist standards that were not reasonable for the popular press.

In May 1973, at a panel discussion that was part of the Second A. J. Liebling Counter-Convention held in Washington, D.C., and sponsored by [More], M. J. Roussant of the Twentieth Century Fund argued that he did not expect the council to work miracles, but that it deserved to be given a chance. He said the council would provide access to the public, would defend freedom of information and the press, would make editors more careful, should raise public awareness, and would praise when praise is justified.

The Twentieth Century Fund could draw upon several antecedents in shaping its national council: the proposal of the Hutchins Commission for a national council, and the British Press Council, an outgrowth of a study by a Royal Commission on the Press appointed in 1947, as well as the newly established Minnesota Press Council.

The Hutchins Commission had recommended:

> some agency which reflects the ambitions of the American people for its press should exist for the purpose of comparing the accomplishments of the press with the aspirations which the people have for it . . . [and] would also educate the people as to the aspirations which they ought to have for the press.[13]

The commission proposed the agency be created by gifts, be independent of government and of the press, and be given a ten-year trial until its own achievement could be audited. The commission suggested that the agency's activities include:

1. Continuing efforts, through conference with practitioners and analysis by its staff, to help the press define workable standards of performance, a task on which our Commission has attempted a beginning.

2. Pointing out the inadequacy of press service in certain areas and the trend toward concentration in others, to the end that local communities and press itself may organize to supply service where it is lacking or to provide alternative service where the drift toward monopoly seems dangerous.

3. Inquiries in areas where minority groups are excluded from reasonable access to the channels of communication.

4. Inquiries abroad regarding the picture of American life presented by the American press; and cooperation with agencies in other countries and with international agencies engaged in analysis of communication across national borders.

5. Investigation of instances of press lying, with particular reference to persistent misrepresentation of the data required for judging public issues.

6. Periodic appraisal of the tendencies and characteristics of the various branches of the communications industry.

7. Continuous appraisal of governmental action affecting communications.

8. Encouragement of the establishment of centers of advanced study, research, and criticism in the field of communications at universities.

9. Encouragement of projects which give hope of meeting the needs of special audiences.

10. The widest possible publicity and public discussion on all the foregoing.[14]

While the commission recommended five ideals for society in evaluating its press (see discussion in chapter 1), it also outlined what it saw as the failings of the then contemporary press. It reported:

> . . . the development of the press as an instrument of
> mass communication has greatly decreased the
> proportion of the people who can express their opinions
> and ideas through the press.
>
> . . . the few who are able to use the machinery of
> the press as an instrument of mass communication have
> not provided a service adequate to the needs of the
> society.
>
> . . . those who direct the machinery of the press
> have engaged from time to time in practices which the
> society condemns and which, if continued, it will
> inevitably undertake to regulate or control.[15]

The report of the Hutchins Commission came at the very
dawn of the development of television as a major social
influence, including the development of television news
broadcasting. Consequently, it devoted little attention to
broadcast news. Moreover, then as now, the broadcast media
are monitored by the Federal Communications Commission
to the extent that the airwaves, which are public property,
are not misused. The Hutchins Commission was acutely
aware that no similar body existed even to monitor the print
media, and certainly not to regulate it.

The Royal Commission that set out to investigate the
finances, control, management, and ownership of the press
in Great Britain in 1947 did so in a troubled national
atmosphere, one that the Twentieth Century Fund noted in
its own proposal for a national press council:

> Immediately after World War II, Britain was shaken by
> political and social dissonance similar to that of the
> United States today. Press mergers, closings, and
> allegations of sensationalism and slanting of news
> generated public concern and debate in and out of
> Parliament.[16]

The British government's official version of the
establishment of the first Royal Commission on the Press

reported that the trend toward monopoly had generated public concern that the "channels of dissemination would be diminished, the presentation of news become over-selective and the expression of opinion insufficiently diverse."

The Royal Commission's report came out in 1949, but it was not until mid-1953 that the national press council was established. During the whole period of investigation and, subsequently, of working out the role and function of the council, the British press was less than gracious in its acceptance of the idea of the council. In reporting reaction in 1948, for example, *World Press News* ran articles such as "Readers May 'Report' Editors When Letters Not Published," "Newsmen Do Not Agree on Need for a Press Council," and "Advice to Royal Commission: 'Spend a Fortnight in a Newspaper Office,' Says Griffiths."

The British Press Council as originally established was comprised of 25 journalists, 10 representing management and 15 representing editorial staffs at lesser levels. The report of the Royal Commission had at first proposed that lay persons hold membership, but, in hammering out the shape of the council with British press associations and with others, lay persons were omitted. In its early years, the complaints most frequently received by the Press Council involved invation of privacy, violations of good taste, and emphasis on sex.[17]

The continued trend toward monopoly in Britain led to the establishment of a second Royal Commission in 1961, to focus on questions of economic and financial structure of the British press. While neither commission uncovered conclusive evidence that monopoly or concentration was leading to suppression of diverse public opinion, the second commission recommended the reconstitution of the Press Council to include a chairman qualified in law and the inclusion of citizen members with no connection with the press. The second commission also recommended a Press Amalgamations Court to study newspaper transactions, a recommendation at least partly fulfilled by the Monopolies and Mergers Act of 1965, which requires that transfer of large newspapers be accomplished only after consent is gained from the Department of Trade and Industry.

The reconstituted Press Council emerged with 5 lay members; 20 professional members representing various newspaper societies, guilds, and institutes; and an independent chairman of public eminence not connected with the press.

The objectives of the British Press Council are:

1. To preserve the established freedom of the British Press.

2. To maintain the character of the British Press in accordance with the highest professional and commercial standards.

3. To consider complaints about the conduct of the Press or the conduct of persons and organisations towards the Press, to deal with these complaints in whatever manner seems practical and appropriate, and to record resultant action.

4. To keep under review developments likely to restrict the supply of information of public interest and importance.

5. To report publicly on developments that may tend towards greater concentration or monopoly in the Press (including changes in ownership, control and growth of Press undertakings) and to publish statistical information relating thereto.

6. To make representations on appropriate occasions to the Government, organs of the United Nations and to Press organisations overseas.

7. To publish periodical reports recording the council's work and to review, from time to time, developments in the Press and the factors affecting them.

A summary of one year of British Press Council operation revealed 385 complaints against newspapers which, with 19 brought forward from the previous year, made a total of 404 under review. Of these, the council adjudicated in 61 of the cases, upholding 25 and rejecting 36. At year's end, 19 still were in process of investigation, 27 had been disallowed on preliminary investigation and 26 after more thorough examination, 54 were withdrawn, and 223 were not pursued. Causes for complaints included misleading or inaccurate headlines, exaggerated or inaccurate reporting, failure to distinguish between speculation and fact, misrepresentation, the rejection or alteration of letters to the editor, and the subject matter of newspaper pictures.

Earlier press councils of this nature, while nonexistent in America, were not uncommon abroad. The first such body in Europe was founded in 1919 by the Publicists' Club, the Swedish Journalists' Union, and the Swedish Newspaper Publishers' Association as the Press Fair Practices Commission to deal with matters of sound journalistic practices. It was reorganized in 1969 to include representatives of the general public. The reorganization also led in the same year to the establishment of a General Public's Press Ombudsman, to serve as a commissioner of grievances and to prosecute violations of press ethics. Since the Swedish council first was formed, about fifteen other European nations have formed press councils.[18]

Opponents of the national press council in the United States occasionally have pointed to wartime censorship bureaus as examples of what a national council would become. The two principal experiences with wartime censorship, in the two world wars, did not see development of anything that could be called a press council in the contemporary sense.

A week after the United States declared war in 1918, President Woodrow Wilson established a Committee on Public Information. Although the committee, headed by former newsman George Creel, issued a modest code for voluntary newspaper self-censorship, the committee proved to be a public relations tool for the United States, and not a press council. A press council was not needed for the war effort; patriotic editors generally exceeded the not-so-stringent prohibitions of the code. Although some allegations of censorship of the press were made, they proved to be the exception. Even without the code, the Espionage Act of 1917, the Trading-With-the-Enemy Act of 1917, and the Sedition Act of 1918 provided broad powers to government in interpretation of acts of disloyalty. A few newsmen were imprisoned under the Espionage Act for disloyal articles; some newspapers lost mailing privileges.

Within two weeks after the bombing of Pearl Harbor, President Roosevelt created the U.S. Office of Censorship and its director, Byron Price, Associated Press executive news editor, produced a Code of Wartime Practices for the American Press the following month. It warned against improper publication of news such as war production, armaments, weather, fortifications, troop movements, and shipping. The office ceased operation shortly after the surrender of Japan and, as in the case of World War I, had received the patriotic support of the nation's press. Similarly, the Office of Censorship was a far cry from the proposals of the Hutchins Commission, the British Press Council, the Twentieth Century Fund, and others.

Shortly after the Hutchins report was released, and while the first Royal Commission still was in study, a joint Council of Research of the American Association of Schools and Departments of Journalism and the American Association of Teachers of Journalism (now the Association for Education in Journalism) reported its plan for evaluating communication agencies.

It was responding to a 1947 resolution calling for a study to evaluate the performance of the communication agencies during 1948 and succeeding years, in effect a plan for a national study of the performance of the press. While the council found more problems than solutions, it did present a proposal for a way to begin, a beginning that never occurred. In short, the council proposed a system of sampling newspapers and radio stations in cooperation with university journalism schools willing to participate in regional pilot studies. The basic question to be asked was, "How effectively does this [newspaper] serve the people of its community?" In its report, the council observed:

> We will wish to determine how well a newspaper performs its functions to enlighten and to entertain readers, as well as to promote the business life of its area. This must be studied at firsthand against the background of the social, economic, political, and religious life of the newspaper's community, a totally unique composite in every case.[19]

If it was not an instance of euthanasia, it was an instance of press-council infant mortality. Universities and colleges offered little or no support, particularly because cost was a problem, and the proposal died aborning. It was one of many starts and spasms that defined domestic calls for press councils, particularly national press councils.

In 1967, again meeting in Colorado, the AEJ held two panel discussions on criticism of the press which were seen as a "full airing of the problems and issues for the development of opinion upon which the [appropriate committee] can take action next year."[20] The discussions, which included mention of a national press council, did not lead to the establishment of one.

In 1968, a committee of laymen and newsmen, meeting in Washington, D.C., under the sponsorship of the National Institute for Public Affairs, began planning for a national press council that was never to materialize under its aegis.

In 1969 ASNE President Norman Isaacs' proposal for a national grievance committee to handle substantial criticism of journalism was turned aside when the ASNE decided instead to establish a committee to study the ethics of the press, a study that led to the already-mentioned poll of editors.

Also in 1969, the study force of the National Commission on the Causes and Prevention of Violence suggested the establishment of an independent Center for Media Study with a governing board of prominent nonpolitical and nonmedia persons selected by the President of the United States. The study force also recommended that the President appoint a Media Advisory Board made up of journalists and a Research Board composed of scholars in law, social sciences, management, economics, psychiatry, and communications technology.

The press council as both concept and institution promises to endure in the several Western societies that find it useful. In the United States, the best use for a national council may be that suggested by the (Hutchins) Commission on a Free and Responsible Press, the reconciliation of the ambitions of society with its aspirations for its press. If a national press council exists to improve the press, it exists more emphatically to improve the relationship between the press and society. Sure and absolute cures for head colds and the problems of society are hard come by, and a national press council is unlikely to prove a panacea or a Xanadu. Even so, the existence of one offers a valuable opportunity to explore and perhaps improve the relationship shared by society and its press.

5 EPILOGUE
AND ORWELL

Criticism affirms the stature and importance of its subject. Like imitation, it is a sincere form of flattery. Criticism often is abused; too often what is passed off as criticism is superficial, self-aggrandizing pap or mere carping. But, when it is informed, thoughtful, and honest, it can be a powerful social force. U.S. Supreme Court Justice Felix Frankfurter once declared, "Criticism is the spur to reform; and Burke's admonition that a healthy society must reform in order to conserve has not lost its force. . . ."[1] This is the notion that overarches this small study of criticism of the press. Criticism articulates standards, ideals, and values. It is generative, not destructive. It mediates where values conflict, when the criticism is public. Where criticism is limited to confreres, it cannot mediate the values of society. Criticism is based on standards and values as it creates new ones. It is a definitive factor for correction. It is the difference that can make a difference. Morris L. Ernst, a New York attorney who contributes regularly to the *Villager*, a New York City weekly, and who is the author of *The First Freedom* (1946) has written:

> I happen to hold with our founding fathers that criticism is the single greatest corrective known to man. In this thesis lies the difference between dictatorships—of the left or right—and the few free societies of our planet.[2]

There are, of course, differences that matter and differences that do not. From just and unjust criticisms, from valid and invalid cries for criticism, the press too often has run for the shelter of the First Amendment. A number of critics have observed the "cry wolf" aspect of this response, a response that has the final effect of making easier the predation of the wolf. While there is shelter from governmental intervention in the First Amendment, there is no shelter from society itself or from the derogation of society. Moreover, rain falls equally upon the just and the unjust; so does criticism, and so it should. It affirms the just and corrects the unjust. The First Amendment guarantees freedom of the press, but it does not guarantee its own perpetuity. As is any part of the Constitution, it is amendable.

Considering an alteration of the First Amendment is akin to thinking the unthinkable thought. But, while by no means is it unthinkable, it is neither impossible nor inevitable. Therein lies one of the strongest arguments for vital, affective criticism of the press. Professor Barron's arguments for a new interpretation of the First Amendment to guarantee access to the press is merely a symptom of the problem. More than twenty years earlier, the (Hutchins) Commission on a Free and Responsible Press observed in one chilling paragraph:

Our society requires agencies of mass communication. They are great concentrations of private power. If they are irresponsible, not even the First Amendment will protect their freedom from governmental control. The amendment will be amended.[3]

The report continued with the assertion that those interested in a free press should do what they can do to ensure that the press is accountable to society, which is what criticism is all about.

It is true that there is a sense of "grand purpose" about journalism, and it is true that the grand purpose relates to the preservation of a free people in a political state. The objections raised by journalists when the National News Council was established point to the concern that criticism, at least formal, institutional criticism, threatens the successful prosecution of that purpose. The alternative proposition is that nothing could serve it better than effective, public, formal criticism.

There are at least two principal considerations in analyzing questions about press criticism. One may seem less real than the other, but points in no lesser way to the necessity that the press enjoy the respect and affection of society.

First, the tradition of anti-utopian literature has worked its way into the warp and the woof of contemporary thought. Aldous Huxley and *Brave New World*, Eugene Zamiatin and *We*, Jack London and *The Iron Heel*, and George Orwell and *1984* are among the best-known examples.

In Orwell, whose *1984* is the most recent and most influential of these anti-utopian works, it is a "thoughtcrime" to write in a personal diary, to say nothing of writing for a newspaper, magazine, or broadcast station. The book depicts a society with no independent activities or enterprises in the helpless grasp of an all-powerful state. It thus suggests a point made earlier here that basic changes in society are neither inevitable nor impossible. How enduring such a concept is may be seen in John Adams' attempt to control the press through the Alien and Sedition Acts, as well as his observation in 1815 that "regulation of the press is the most difficult, dangerous and important problem [philosophers, politicians, and others] have to resolve. Mankind cannot now be governed without it, nor at present with it."

The second major consideration leads from the first: the press is in Milton's envisioned arena where truth does battle with falsehood or error, even if too often the latter may be attributed to the press. The press also is in an arena in which it contests with other powerful forces in society. The confrontation between the administration of President Richard Nixon and the press became the most spectacular such encounter of modern times. Directly and indirectly, both sought the loyalty of the public in pursuing what was to become more than the traditional press-government adversary roles.

Then-Vice-President Spiro Agnew challenged the credibility of the press in speech and memo during Nixon's first term in office. He was supported by a large White House staff in what proved to be a well-orchestrated campaign to improve or restore the image of the Nixon administration at the expense of the image of the print and broadcast press. At one period in 1969, President Nixon reportedly wrote more than twenty memos in thirty days complaining to his aides about adverse press coverage. If there was a balance among adversaries, it was destroyed in 1972 as Nixon's triumphant reelection campaign drew to a close. What was to become a scandal of staggering proportions broke in front pages across the country after it was discovered that burglars associated with Nixon's reelection campaign had established electronic bugging of the National Democratic Headquarters in the Watergate Hotel in Washington. The scandal reached to the threshold of the President's office after a score of presidential aides, two cabinet members, and others had fallen by the political wayside. Watergate involved the President's personal staff in charges of lying, of planting false accusations of racism and homosexuality against opponents, and of illegal and unethical payoffs and coverups.

Congressional, administrative, and other investigative agencies also uncovered White House attempts to intimidate and discredit what it saw as an unfair, inaccurate, and hostile press. The clamor for impeachment or resignation grew. Nixon, who denied involvement in any wrongdoing, also announced and reannounced his distrust of the media and his lack of respect for nationally known journalists. The controversy grew even sharper after the resignation of Agnew and his plea of no contest to income tax evasion.

The Watergate story was for many a triumph for journalism. Dogged, determined investigative reporting broke down an imposing wall of government secrecy, leak by leak, revealing scandal after scandal. It earned a Pulitzer Prize for the Washington *Post* which had led the nation's press in developing the story. For others, however, Watergate was not a journalistic hallmark. Some, even some journalists, saw the hunting hounds of the press more as a pack of jackals biting at the heart of American institutions. One organization, the National Citizens' Committee for Fairness to the Presidency, said in one of a series of paid ads in major newspapers that, "The media have found President Richard M. Nixon guilty! They scandalized him, they brutalized him, they savaged him day after day, night after night, and now they have come to bury him, draped in infamy, with the White House for a coffin."

Poll after national poll indicated a decline in Nixon's popularity. But if Watergate was a triumph for the press over a skillful and powerful adversary, it was not so seen by a large segment of the public. It is important to note that both contestants in the arena bore the scars of battle.

The first opinion poll ever commissioned by Congress showed in late 1973 that the executive branch of the federal government ranked last in public confidence of ten institutions; it also showed that the press ranked eighth, but that television news ranked third.[4]

Included in the Louis Harris poll were medicine, higher education, television news, the military, organized religion, the U.S. Supreme Court, the U.S. Senate, the press, major corporations, and the executive branch. The question asked aimed at popular trust in the leaders of these major institutions.

The poll indicated that of these, only the executive branch fell below the 1972 trust level. It indicated that, while the press rebounded over its 1972 trust level, it did so only to about the 1966 trust level (about 30 percent). Television news alone among the measured institutions surpassed the 1966 trust level.

Harris concluded from the study, which indicated that most people believed something seriously wrong with America, that, "In this unhappy verdict is summed up the broad loss of confidence, the pervasive sense of discontent and the most serious reasons for concern about the future course of democracy." [5]

If the Harris poll did not show the press in a confidence crisis, it did show it in a lack of confidence predicament at what may become a crucial time. The last quarter of the twentieth century may see cosmic changes in the problems to be faced by all mankind, not only in political and communication systems. It is possible to anticipate an endless energy crisis, irreversible pollution, and a massive population explosion.

With the population explosion seems to run problems of violence, particularly in urban areas, and widespread political pluralism with the accompanying breakdown of societal consensus on political, social, economic, and moral issues. These may prove to be vital problems; political states will deal with them because it will be necessary to deal with at least some of them.

When societies adjust to meet massive and serious challenges, the changes generated in social systems frequently are correspondingly massive. If it does not prove fortunate, it will prove ironic that these problems threaten to occur at a time of unparalleled scientific and technological capacity to solve them. Yet, scientific and technological capacities introduce different problems, some more direct to journalism. While the cathode ray tube may make it commonplace to set into print thousands of words a minute, the advent of cable television may multiply by ten or more the number of television channels available to every home. Similarly, video-audio home recorders may become as commonplace as the television sets to which they would be linked. These developments cannot but hold vast changes for journalism, particularly when they are taken in chorus.

It seems fair to predict that traditions and traditional ways are going to have to meet new challenges in the not-too-distant future, and some of the challenges may harbor implications for the fundamental structures of society, including the First Amendment. It is possible to envisage a shift from democratic ideal to one of functional utility for society, a shift that could bring to question all the institutions of society, including the press in its several forms. If journalists have chosen the First Amendment as first and last refuge when threatened, there is in this an element of nescience. The First Amendment is not the vital refuge; the goodwill of society is. And this is what criticism of the press is all about. The future may hold a host of bogeymen, some of them real and some of them not. Since there is no way to tell which is which, it behooves the press, to coin an odious cliché, to hope for the best and prepare for the worst. One way to forestall the worst is to become the willing, even eager subject of the criticism of society. Ben Bagdikian once observed, writing about racial balance on the staff of the Washington *Post*, that to be the best may not be good enough. This is equally true of the institutions of society.

Perhaps no institution of society has been subjected to more searching criticism and self-criticism as the news-gathering institution, but, if public confidence is the criterion, the criticism has been either inadequate or impotent. Another factor is that the press has done a dismal job of taking society into its confidence in making public its failings, problems, successes, and improvements. More than anything else, this may contribute to what seems to be a widespread feeling of "apart from" instead of "a part of."

Historically, criticism of the press has been of uneven quality and inwardly directed. Where the response has been positive, the public rarely has been directly told about it. Instead, improvements have usually been presented with little fanfare. When there has been revelation of progress, as in the case of the automotive industry, it has tended to emphasize trim instead of substance, or promotion instead of product.

Some great newspapers set superb standards for accuracy, completeness, responsibility, meaning, and usefulness. Most do not, but fall somewhat short. If their consumers also find them so, it may be assumed that their vital friends are fewer rather than more, and that they are not meeting the needs of society. Peculiarly, it is more difficult to identify a great newscast, perhaps because the visual image and the spoken word are fleeting; more, they leave no artifact of their having been, except in memory, which may be trusted only with reservation.

There remain more questions than answers about press criticism. There are too few issues about it. The most basic issue involves whether or not to have formal, institutional criticism of the press. If so, a corollary issue involves who, what, where, and how?

—Shall the critics be journalists or others?
—Who are journalists who are qualified to criticize? Or, who want to?

—What can formal public criticism do that responsible enlightened media units are not already accomplishing?

—Does the press need more criticism at a time when it already is being criticized from every quarter?

—Why should the press willingly cooperate with an institution, such as a national press council, that could threaten rights guaranteed by the First Amendment?

—What form of criticism is most productive—accuracy forms, journals of criticism, ombudsmen, local or national press councils?

Regardless of the answer to any of these questions, the fact remains that the press requires criticism as an ongoing activity as do all of society's institutions. Reform should be an equally ongoing activity, and the public should be apprised of it. Moreover, the press requires criticism to generate improvement sufficient to meet society's requirements. The national press council and other institutions for criticism of the press pose little or no threat to First Amendment guarantees. A national council or other institution for criticism has no coercive power, unless publication and publicity is coercive. The extent of publicity, of course, will be determined in large part by those who own the presses. In substance, criticism in whatever form can only serve as a bulwark for First Amendment rights. But, as Adlai Stevenson said in accepting the nomination for President in 1952, "There are no gains without pains."

What may be needed finally is a national organization not to criticize the press, but to guide and criticize the critics. While individual publishers and station owners would finance an ombudsman, a press council, the use of accuracy forms, or an exchange journalist in cooperation with another publisher or station owner, such a national body might be financed by foundations, press associations, or by professional and academic organizations. Institutional criticism of the press thus far has been a lonely, even isolated activity. Such an association or institution could collect, analyze, distribute, publicize, and attempt to guide the activities of the critics or the critical vehicles. While it is true that each media unit operates in an unique environment, it is equally true that people are much the same everywhere. An effect of such a system could be to secure useful insight into what the public does demand of its journalists, and through the sharing of such information, to expand and facilitate the dialogue between society and the press.

Moderation and facilitation of the dialogue between society and the mass media is the goal of all press criticism worthy of the name. The objective simply is to aid the press in serving society and to aid society in causing the press to better meet its needs. Alienation cannot work to the benefit of either press or society. To remain free and to fulfill whatever societal meaning it may have, the press must be both responsible and responsive. This is the functional purpose of press criticism.

Appendix A
CODES OF ETHICS

The ethics of the press may, in part, be judged by ethical standards of its own creation and adoption. Included here is the Code of Ethics adopted by the American Society of Newspaper Editors in 1923 (Canons of Journalism); the Code of Broadcast News Ethics adopted in 1966 by the Radio Television News Directors Association; the Kansas Code of Ethics, adopted by the Kansas Editorial Association in 1910 and believed to be the earliest code of ethics adopted by any association of journalists. Also included are several early codes of ethics adopted by individual newspapers; with the Kansas Code of Ethics, they were incorporated in Nelson A. Crawford's *The Ethics of Journalism* (New York: Appleton-Century-Crofts, 1924) and are reprinted with permission of the publisher. The Code of Ethics of The Society of Professional Journalists, Sigma Delta Chi, which is included in this appendix, was adopted in national convention in 1973.

101

THE CANONS OF JOURNALISM
American Society of Newspaper Editors

The primary function of newspapers is to communicate to the human race what its members do, feel, and think. Journalism, therefore, demands of its practitioners the widest range of intelligence or knowledge and of experience, as well as natural and trained powers of observation and reasoning. To its opportunities as a chronicle are indissolubly linked its obligations as teacher and interpreter.

To the end of finding some means of codifying sound practice and just aspirations of American journalism, these canons are set forth:

I

Responsibility. The right of a newspaper to attract and hold readers is restricted by nothing but considerations of public welfare. The use a newspaper makes of the share of public attention it gains serves to determine its sense of responsibility, which it shares with every member of its staff. A journalist who uses his power for any selfish or otherwise unworthy purpose is faithless to a high trust.

II

Freedom of the Press. Freedom of the press is to be guarded as a vital right of mankind. It is the unquestionable right to discuss whatever is not explicitly forbidden by law, including the wisdom of any restrictive statute.

III

Independence. Freedom from all obligations except that of fidelity to the public interest is vital.

1. Promotion of any private interest contrary to the general welfare, for whatever reason, is not compatible with honest journalism. So-called news communications from private sources should not be published without public notice of their source or else substantiation of their claims to value as news, both in form and substance.

2. Partisanship, in editorial comment which knowingly departs from the truth, does violence to the best spirit of American journalism; in the news columns it is subversive of a fundamental principle of the profession.

IV

Sincerity, Truthfulness, Accuracy. Good faith with the reader is the foundation of all journalism worthy of the name.

1. By every consideration of good faith a newspaper is constrained to be truthful. It is not to be excused for lack of thoroughness or accuracy within its control, or failure to obtain command of these essential qualities.

2. Headlines should be fully warranted by the contents of the article which they surmount.

V

Impartiality. Sound practice makes clear distinction between news reports and expressions of opinion. News reports should be free from opinion or bias of any kind.

1. This rule does not apply to so-called special articles unmistakably devoted to advocacy or characterized by a signature authorizing the writer's own conclusions and interpretation.

VI

Fair Play. A newspaper should not publish official charges affecting reputation or moral character without opportunity given to the accused to be heard; right practice demands the giving of such opportunity in all cases of serious accusation outside judicial proceedings.

1. A newspaper should not invade private rights or feelings without sure warrant of public right as distinguished from public curiosity.

2. It is the privilege, as it is the duty, of a newspaper to make prompt and complete correction of its own serious mistakes of fact or opinion, whatever their origin.

VII

Decency. A newspaper cannot escape conviction of insincerity if while professing high moral purpose it supplies incentives to base conduct, such as are to be found in details of crime and vice, publication of which is not demonstrably for the general good. Lacking authority to enforce its canons, the journalism here represented can but express the hope that deliberate panderings to vicious instincts will encounter effective public disapproval or yield to the influence of a preponderant professional condemnation.

CODE OF BROADCAST NEWS ETHICS
Radio Television News Directors Association

The following Code of Broadcast News Ethics for RTNDA was adopted January 2, 1966.

The members of the Radio Television News Directors Association agree that their prime responsibility as newsmen—and that of the broadcasting industry as the collective sponsor of news broadcasting—is to provide to the public they serve a news service as accurate, full and prompt as human integrity and devotion can devise. To that end, they declare their acceptance of the standards of practice here set forth, and their solemn intent to honor them to the limits of their ability.

Article One

The primary purpose of broadcast newsmen—to inform the public of events of importance and appropriate interest in a manner that is accurate and comprehensive—shall override all other purposes.

Article Two

Broadcast news presentations shall be designed not only to offer timely and accurate information, but also to present it in the light of relevant circumstances that give it meaning and perspective.

> This standard means that news reports, when clarity demands it, will be laid against pertinent factual background; that factors such as race, creed, nationality or prior status will be reported only when they are relevant; that comment or subjective content will be properly identified; and that errors in fact will be promptly acknowledged and corrected.

Article Three

Broadcast newsmen shall seek to select material for newscast solely on their evaluation of its merits as news.

> This standard means that news will be selected on the criteria of significance, community and regional relevance, appropriate human interest, service to defined audiences. It excludes sensationalism or misleading emphasis in any form; subservience to external or "interested" efforts to influence news selection and presentation, whether from within the broadcasting industry or from without. It requires that such terms as "bulletin" and "flash" be used only when the character of the news justifies them; that bombastic or misleading descriptions of newsroom facilities and personnel be rejected, along with undue use of sound and visual effects; and that promotional or publicity material be sharply scrutinized before use and identified by source or otherwise when broadcast.

Article Four

Broadcast newsmen shall at all times display humane respect

for the dignity, privacy and the well-being of persons with whom the news deals.

Article Five

Broadcast newsmen shall govern their personal lives and such nonprofessional associations as may impinge on their professional activities in a manner that will protect them from conflict of interest, real or apparent.

Article Six

Broadcast newsmen shall seek actively to present all news the knowledge of which will serve the public interest, no matter what selfish, uninformed or corrupt efforts attempt to color it, withhold it or prevent its presentation. They shall make constant effort to open doors closed to the reporting of public proceedings with tools appropriate to broadcasting (including cameras and recorders), consistent with the public interest. They acknowledge the newsman's ethic of protection of confidential information and sources, and urge unswerving observation of it except in instances in which it would clearly and unmistakably defy the public interest.

Article Seven

Broadcast newsmen recognize the responsibility borne by broadcasting for informed analysis, comment and editorial opinion on public events and issues. They accept the obligation of broadcasters, for the presentation of such matters by individuals whose competence, experience and judgment qualify them for it.

Article Eight

In court, broadcast newsmen shall conduct themselves with dignity, whether the court is in or out of session. They shall keep broadcast equipment as unobtrusive and silent as possible. Where court facilities are inadequate, pool broadcasts should be arranged.

Article Nine

In reporting matters that are or may be litigated, the

newsman shall avoid practices which would tend to interfere with the right of an individual to a fair trial.

Article Ten

Broadcast newsmen shall actively censure and seek to prevent violations of these standards, and shall actively encourage their observance by all newsmen, whether of the Radio Television News Directors Association or not.

KANSAS CODE OF ETHICS [1]

For the Publisher

In Advertising

Definition. Advertising is news, or views, of a business or professional enterprise which leads directly to its profits or increased business.

News of the industrial or commercial development of an institution which in no way has a specific bearing upon the merits of its products is not advertising.

Besides news which leads to a profit, advertising also includes communications and reports, cards of thanks, etc., over the space of which the editor has no control. Charges for the latter become more in the nature of a penalty to restrict their publication.

Responsibility. The authorship of an advertisement should be so plainly stated in the contract or at the end that it could not avoid catching the attention of the reader before he has left the matter.

Unsigned advertisements in the news columns should either be preceded or followed by the word "advertisement" or its abbreviation.

[1] Written by Willis E. Miller and adopted by the Kansas Editorial Association in 1910—apparently the earliest code of ethics adopted by any association of journalists.

Freedom of Space. We hold the right of the publisher to become a broker in land, loan, rental, and mercantile transactions through his want and advertising columns, and condemn any movement of those following such lines to restrict this right of the publisher to the free sale of his space for the purpose of bringing buyer and seller together.

This shall not be construed to warrant the publisher as such in handling the details, terms, etc., of the trade, but merely in safeguarding his freedom in selling his space to bring the buyer and seller together, leaving the bargaining to the principals.

Our advertising is to bring together the buyer and the seller, and we are not concerned whether it is paid for and ordered by the producer, the consumer, or a middleman.

Acceding to any other desires on the part of traders is knocking the foundations out from under the advertising business—the freedom of space. We hold that the freedom of space (where the payment is not a question) should only be restricted by the moral decency of the advertising matter.

We hold that the freedom of space denies us the right to sign any contract with a firm which contains any restrictions against the wording of the copy which we may receive from any other firm, even to the mentioning of the goods of the first firm by name.

Compensation. We condemn the signing of contracts carrying with them the publication of any amount of free reading matter.

We condemn the acceptance of any exchange articles, trade checks, or courtesies in payment for advertising, holding that all advertising should be paid for in cash.

We condemn the giving of secret rebates upon the established advertising rate as published.

Rates. All advertising rates should be on a unit per thousand basis and all advertisers are entitled to a full knowledge of the circulation, not only of the quantity but also of the distribution. Statements of circulation should show the number of bona fide subscribers, the number of exchanges, the number of complimentaries, and the number sold to newsdealers, and if possible the locality of distribution, in a general way.

Position. Position contracts should be charged a fixed percentage above the established rate of the paper, and no contracts should be signed wherein a failure to give the position required results in a greater reduction from the established rate than the position premium is greater than the established rate.

Comparisons. We consider it beneath the dignity of a publisher to place in his columns statements which make invidious comparisons between the amount of advertising carried or the circulation of his paper and that of his competitor.

Press Agents and Unpaid Advertising. The specific trade name of an article of commerce, or the name of a merchant, manufacturer, or professional man *with reference* to his wares, products, or labors should not be mentioned in a pure news story.

We condemn as against *moral decency* the publication of any advertisement which will obviously lead to any form of retrogression, such as private medical personals, indecent massage parlor advertisements, private matrimonial advertisements, physician's or hospital's advertisement for the care of private diseases, which carry in them any descriptive or suggestive matter of the same.

In Circulation

Definition. Circulation is the entire list of first-hand readers of a publication and comprises the paid readers, complimentary readers, exchange readers, and advertising readers.

Compensation. Subscriptions should be solicited and received only on a basis of cash consideration, the paper and its payment being the only elements to the transaction.

Newsdealers. The purchase of a quantity of papers should be made outright, allowing for no return of unsold copies.

Gambling. We condemn the practice of securing subscriptions through the sale or gift of chances.

Complimentaries. Complimentary copies should not be sent to doctors, lawyers, ministers, postal clerks, police or court officials for news or mailing privileges.

In Estimating

Definition. Estimating is the science of computing costs. Its conclusion is the price.

Basis. We do not favor the establishment of a minimum rate card for advertising which would be uniform among publishers, but we do favor a more thorough understanding of the subject of costs, and commend to our members the labors of the American Printers' Cost Commission of the First International Cost Congress recently held in Chicago. Let us learn our costs and then each establish a rate card based upon our investment and the cost of production, having no consideration for the comparative ability of the advertisers to pay, or the semi-news nature of the advertisement.

Quantity Discount. We consider it unwise to allow discounts greater than 10 percent from the rate of first insertion for succeeding insertions.

News

Definition. News is the impartial report of the activities of mind, men, and matter which do not offend the moral sensibilities of the more enlightened people.

Lies. We condemn as against truth:
1. The publication of fake illustrations of men and events of news interest, however marked their similarity, without an accompanying statement that they are not real pictures of the event or person, but only suggestive imitations.

2. The publication of fake interviews made up of the assumed views of an individual, without his consent.

3. The publication of interviews in quotations unless the exact, approved language of the interviewed be used. When an interview is not an exact quotation it should be obvious in the reading that *only* the thought and impression of the interviewer is being reported.

4. The issuance of fake news dispatches, whether the same have for their purpose the influencing of stock quotations, elections, or the sale of securities or merchandise. Some of the greatest advertising in the world has been stolen through news columns in the form of dispatches from unscrupulous press agents. Millions have been made on the rise and fall of stock quotations caused by newspaper lies, sent out by designing reporters.

Injustice. We condemn as against justice:

1. The practice of reporters making detectives and spies of themselves in their endeavors to investigate the guilt or innocence of those under suspicion.

Reporters should not enter the domain of law in the apprehension of criminals. They should not become a detective or sweating agency for the purpose of furnishing excitement to the readers.

No suspect should have his hope of a just liberty foiled through the great prejudice which the public has formed against him because of the press verdict slyly couched in the news report, even before his arrest.

We should not even by insinuation interpret as facts our conclusions, unless by signature we become personally responsible for them. Exposition, explanation, and interpretation should be left to the field of the expert or specialist with a full consciousness of his personal responsibility.

2. The publication of the rumors and common gossips or the assumptions of a reporter relative to a suspect pending his arrest or the final culmination of his trial. A staff of reporters is not a detective agency, and the right of a suspect to a fair and impartial trial is often confounded by a

reporter's practice of printing every ill-founded rumor of which he gets wind.

Incedencies. Classification: For the sake of clearness and order, crimes with which we will be concerned may be divided into those which offend against the *public trust* (such as bribery, defalcation, or embezzlement by a public official); those which offend against *private institutions* or *employers* (which are also often defalcations and betrayals of confidence), and crimes which offend against *private morality,* most often centering around the family relation.

1. In dealing with the suspicions against *public officials* or trustees we urge that *only facts* put in their *true relation* and records be used in the news reports.

No presumption or conclusion of the reporter should be allowed to enter, even though it has all the elements of a correct conclusion.

Conclusions and presumptions should be placed in interviews with the identity of their author easily apparent.

If an editor desires to draw a conclusion on the case, let him sign it. Do not hide behind the impersonality of the paper with your personal opinions.

2. In dealing with the suspicions against agents of private institutions, facts alone, put in their true relation, should again be used.

But in this class of stories suspicions and conclusions should be confined to those of the parties directly interested, and no statement of one party to the affair reflecting upon another should be published without at the same time publishing a statement of the accused relative thereto.

The comment of those not directly involved should not be published previous to the arrest or pending the trial.

3. In dealing with the offenses against private morality, we should refuse to print any record of the matter, however true, until the warrant has been filed or the arrest made, and even then our report should contain only an epitome of the charges by the plaintiff and the answers by the defendant, preferably secured from their respective attorneys.

No society gossips or scandals, however true, should ever be published concerning such cases.

However prominent the principals, offenses against private morality should never receive *first-page position* and their details should be eliminated as much as possible.

Certain crimes against private morality which are revolting to our finer sensibilities should be ignored entirely; however, in the event of their having become public with harmful exaggerations, we may make an elementary statement, couched in the least suggestive language.

In no case should the reckless daring of the suspect be lionized.

4. Except when the suspect has escaped, his picture should never be printed.

For the Editor

Views

Definition. Views are the impressions, beliefs, or opinions which are published in a paper, whether from the editorial staffs of the same, outside contributors, or secured interviews.

A Distinction. We hold that whenever a publication confines the bulk of its views to any particular line of thought, class of views, or side of a moot question, it becomes to that extent a class publication, and insomuch ceases to be a newspaper.

An Explanation. You will note by our definition of news that it is the impartial portrayal of the decent activities of mind, men, and matter. This definition applied to class publications would be changed by replacing the word *impartial* with the word *partial*.

In this section we will deal with *impartiality* in the presentation of the decent activities of the mind of the community—with the views or editorial policy of a paper.

Responsibility. Whereas a view or conclusion is the product of some mind or minds, and whereas the value and significance of a view is dependent upon the known merit of its author or authors, the reader is entitled and has the right to know the personal identity of the author, whether by the signature in a communication, the statement of the reporter in an interview, or the caption in a special article, and *the paper as such* should in no wise become an advocate.

Influence (Editorial). We should avoid permitting large institutions or persons to own stock in or make loans to our publishing business if we have reasonable grounds to believe that their interest would be seriously affected by any other than a true presentation of all news and free willingness to present every possible point of view under signature or interview.

Influence (Reportorial). No reporter should be retained who accepts any courtesies, unusual favors, opportunities for self-gain, or side employment from any factors whose interests would be affected by the manner in which his reports are made.

Deception. We should not allow the *presumed* knowledge on the part of the interviewed that we are newspaper men to permit us to quote them without their explicit permission, but where such knowledge is certain we insist upon our right to print the views unless directly forbidden.

Faith With Interviewed. An interview or statement should not be displayed previous to its publication without the permission of the author.

Bounds of Publicity. A man's name and portrait are his private property and the point where they cease to be private and become public should be defined for our association.

THE HEARST NEWSPAPERS [1]

Advertising

The principles and policies governing the advertising department of our newspapers should be just as firmly established and just as well known to every one in the business office as the news and editorial departments.

News and editorial character are built only on reliability of statement. We cannot hope to build advertising on any other basis. No man who misrepresents facts must be allowed on our newspapers. Honesty is a form of common sense.

Employ men of brains, breeding and acquaintance. Character counts in advertising as in all other things.

Our newspapers must sell advertising only by their printed rate card. If your rate card is wrong, change it. If it is right, live up to every letter of it. There should be no double standard of morality involving buyer and seller of advertising. Cut rates, special concessions and secret rebates are boomerangs, which return to cripple progress when they are least expected. Men who make "gentlemen's agreements" are not wanted.

Do not accept any advertising which is detrimental to the public welfare. Questionable financial, objectionable medical, clairvoyants, spiritualists, fortune tellers and fake advertising of any and every description have no place in the Hearst newspapers. Our readers trust us. We would not deceive them in our news or editorial columns. We must not allow others to deceive them in our advertising columns.

News

Make the paper *accurate and trustworthy.*

Compare statements in our paper with those in other papers and find out which are accurate.

---

[1] The selections are from the personal instructions given by William Randolph Hearst to his newspapers.

Get rid of reporters and copy-readers who are persistently inaccurate. Reward those who are trustworthy as you reward those who are valuable in other respects.

Don't allow exaggeration. It is a cheap and ineffective substitute for real interest. Show appreciation for reporters *who can make the truth interesting.* Eliminate those who can not.

Be fair and impartial in the news columns at least. Don't make a paper for Democrats, or Republicans, or Independence Leaguers. Make a paper for all the people, and give unbiased news of all creeds and parties. Try to do this in such a conspicuous manner that it will *be noticed* and *commented* upon.

Condense the news when necessary to get it in. Much of the news is *better* when *intelligently condensed.*

Make your departments complete and reliable, so that the reader will know, first, that he can find a thing in the paper, and, second, that he can find it right.

Make the paper *thorough;* print all the news. Not only get all the news into the office, but see that it gets into the paper.

Select the *best stories* in the paper and *feature* them—i.e., emphasize them in a way to make them stand out and give life and character to the paper.

If your feature is big enough, it must get *display, regardless of everything;* but mere display does not make a feature.

It is *not necessary to cover a page with a story* in order to make it a feature. A page feature generally looks heavy and is heavy. A story should be made to stand out by *appreciation* of the interesting points and *emphasis* of those points in typography and phraseology. A feature *can* be made interesting in a column, and it may be made stupid in a page.

Make a paper *for the best kind of people.* The masses of the reading public are better and more intelligent than newspapermen seem to think they are.

Don't print a lot of stuff that nice people are supposed to like and do not, but omit things that will offend nice people.

Avoid *coarseness* and *slang* and a *low tone*. The most sensational news can be told if it is written properly.

Don't use the words "murder," "scandal," "divorce," "crime," and other rather offensive phrases when it is possible to tell the story without them. Murder stories and other criminal stories are not printed merely because they are *criminal*, but because of the *mystery*, or the *romance*, or the *dramatic qualities* in them. Therefore, develop the *mystery*, or the *romance*, or the *dramatic qualities*, and avoid the offensive qualities.

Make the paper helpful and kindly and pleasing.

Don't scold and forever complain and attack in the news columns.

An occasionally justifiable crusade or exposure will be all the more effective if this rule is maintained.

Please sum up your paper every day at a conference and find wherein it is *distinctly better* than the other papers. If it is not distinctly better, you have *missed that day*. Lay out plans to make it distinctly better the next day.

THE SACRAMENTO BEE

The Bee demands from all its writers accuracy before anything else. Better lose an item than make a splurge one day and correct it next.

Equally with that, it demands absolute fairness in the treatment of news. Reports must not be colored to please a friend or wrong an enemy.

Don't editorialize in the news columns. An accurate report is its own best editorial.

Don't exaggerate. Every exaggeration hurts immeasurably the cause it pretends to help.

If a mistake is made, it must be corrected. It is as much the duty of a *Bee* writer to work to the rectification of a wrong done by an error in an item as it is first to use every precaution not to allow that error to creep in.

Be extremely careful of the name and reputation of

women. Even when dealing with the unfortunate, remember that so long as she commits no crime other than her own sin against chastity, she is entitled at least to pity.

Sneers at race, or religion, or physical deformity, will not be tolerated. "Dago," "Mick," "Sheeny," even "Chink" or "Jap," these are absolutely forbidden. This rule of regard for the feelings of others must be observed in every avenue of news, under any and all conditions.

There is a time for humor and there is a time for seriousness. *The Bee* likes snap and ginger at all times. It will not tolerate flippancy on serious subjects on any occasion.

The furnisher of an item is entitled to a hearing for his side at all times, not championship. If the latter is ever deemed necessary, the editorial department will attend to it.

Interviews given the paper at the paper's request are to be considered immune from sneers or criticism.

In every accusation against a public official or private citizen, make every effort to have the statement of the accused given prominence in the original item.

In the case of charges which are not ex officio or from a public source, it is better to lose an item than to chance the doing of a wrong.

Consider *The Bee* always as a tribunal that desires to do justice to all; that fears far more to do injustice to the poorest beggar than to clash swords with wealthy injustice.

THE SEATTLE TIMES

The following rules of decency are published for the guidance of all concerned:

(a) Remember that young girls read *The Times.*

(b) The physiology of conception and childbirth and all matters relating thereto will not be discussed in the columns of *The Times.*

(c) All scandalous matter will be omitted, excepting where competent orders are given to the contrary.

(d) When it is necessary to refer to improper relations between the sexes, the limit permitted in *The Times* is some such statement as: "The couple were divorced," or "The couple separated," or "Various charges were made not considered fit for publication in the columns of *The Times*."

(e) The use of the words, "rape," "adultery," "indecent exposure," "incest," "assault" (in this connection), or any word, phrase, or sentence, similar or having like meaning, is prohibited.

(f) As far as practicable, any news bearing upon events that depend upon the commission of crimes of sex will be omitted from the paper. Where a person is lynched for a crime against a woman or child, the cause of the lynching will not be given, and for it will be substituted some such statement as "The victim of the mob was accused of injuring a woman."

(g) Reference to expectancy of motherhood or physicians' certificates in connection with establishment of the innocence of a woman charged with a sexual crime, or any other subject that in the remotest degree is of a similar character, will be omitted.

(h) In connection with accidents where persons are injured or killed, all unpleasant details of suffering or maiming will be omitted. In this connection the word "mangle" is forbidden, and this prohibition should carry with it by inference anything of a similar nature.

CODE OF ETHICS

The Society of Professional Journalists, Sigma Delta Chi
(Adopted by the national convention, November 16, 1973)

The Society of Professional Journalists, Sigma Delta Chi, believes the duty of journalists is to serve the truth.
We believe the agencies of mass communication are

carriers of public discussion and information, acting on their Constitutional mandate and freedom to learn and report the facts.

We believe in public enlightenment as the forerunner of justice, and in our Constitutional role to seek the truth as part of the public's right to know the truth.

We believe those responsibilities carry obligations that require journalists to perform with intelligence, objectivity, accuracy, and fairness.

To these ends, we declare acceptance of the standards of practice here set forth:

Responsibility: The public's right to know of events of public importance and interest is the overriding mission of the mass media. The purpose of distributing news and enlightened opinion is to serve the general welfare. Journalists who use their professional status as representatives of the public for selfish or other unworthy motives violate a high trust.

Freedom of the Press: Freedom of the press is to be guarded as an inalienable right of people in a free society. It carries with it the freedom and the responsibility to discuss, question, and challenge actions and utterances of our government and of our public and private institutions. Journalists uphold the right to speak unpopular opinions and the privilege to agree with the majority.

Ethics: Journalists must be free of obligation to any interest other than the public's right to know.

1. Gifts, favors, free travel, special treatment or privileges can compromise the integrity of journalists and their employers. Nothing of value should be accepted.

2. Secondary employment, political involvement, holding public office, and service in community organizations should be avoided if it compromises the integrity of journalists and their employers. Journalists and their employers should conduct their personal lives in a manner which protects them from conflict of interest, real or apparent. Their responsibilities to the public are paramount. That is the nature of their profession.

3. So-called news communications from private sources should not be published or broadcast without substantiation of their claims to news value.

4. Journalists will seek news that serves the public interest, despite the obstacles. They will make constant efforts to assure that the public's business is conducted in public and that public records are open to public inspection.

5. Journalists acknowledge the newsman's ethic of protecting confidential sources of information.

Accuracy and Objectivity: Good faith with the public is the foundation of all worthy journalism.

1. Truth is our ultimate goal.

2. Objectivity in reporting the news is another goal which serves as the mark of an experienced professional. It is a standard of performance toward which we strive. We honor those who achieve it.

3. There is no excuse for inaccuracies or lack of thoroughness.

4. Newspaper headlines should be fully warranted by the contents of the articles they accompany. Photographs and telecasts should give an accurate picture of an event and not highlight a minor incident out of context.

5. Sound practice makes clear distinction between news reports and expressions of opinion. News reports should be free of opinion or bias and represent all sides of an issue.

6. Partisanship in editorial comment which knowingly departs from the truth violates the spirit of American journalism.

7. Journalists recognize their responsibility for offering informed analysis, comment, and editorial opinion on public events and issues. They accept the obligation to present such material by individuals whose competence, experience, and judgment qualify them for it.

8. Special articles or presentations devoted to advocacy or the writer's own conclusions and interpretations should be labeled as such.

Fair Play: Journalists at all times will show respect for the dignity, privacy, rights, and well-being of people encountered in the course of gathering and presenting the news.

1. The news media should not communicate unofficial charges affecting reputation or moral character without giving the accused a chance to reply.

2. The news media must guard against invading a person's right to privacy.

3. The media should not pander to morbid curiosity about details of vice and crime.

4. It is the duty of news media to make prompt and complete correction of their errors.

5. Journalists should be accountable to the public for their reports and the public should be encouraged to voice its grievances against the media. Open dialogue with our readers, viewers, and listeners should be fostered.

Pledge: Journalists should actively censure and try to prevent violations of these standards, and they should encourage their observance by all newspeople. Adherence to this code of ethics is intended to preserve the bond of mutual trust and respect between American journalists and the American people.

Appendix **B**
REPORTS FOR A NATIONAL PRESS COUNCIL

Among the many calls for a national press council are two of particular importance. Included here is part of chapter 6 of the Report of the Commission on Freedom of the Press, "What Can Be Done," from *A Free and Responsible Press*, published in 1947 by The University of Chicago Press. Also included is the Twentieth Century Fund Task Force Report for a National News Council, published in 1973 by the Twentieth Century Fund.

123

FROM REPORT OF THE COMMISSION ON FREEDOM OF THE PRESS *

3. We recommend the establishment of a new and independent agency to appraise and report annually upon the performance of the press.

The public makes itself felt by the press at the present time chiefly through pressure groups. These groups are quite as likely to have bad influence as good. In this field we cannot turn to government as the representative of the people as a whole, and we would not do so if we could. Yet it seems to us clear that some agency which reflects the ambitions of the American people for its press should exist for the purpose of comparing the accomplishments of the press with the aspirations which the people have for it. Such an agency would also educate the people as to the aspirations which they ought to have for the press.

The Commission suggests that such a body be independent of government and of the press; that it be created by gifts; and that it be given a ten-year trial, at the end of which an audit of its achievement could determine anew the institutional form best adapted to its purposes.

The activities of such an agency would include:

1. Continuing efforts, through conference with practitioners and analysis by its staff, to help the press define workable standards of performance, a task on which our Commission has attempted a beginning.

2. Pointing out the inadequacy of press service in certain areas and the trend toward concentration in others, to the end that local communities and the press itself may organize to supply service where it is lacking or to provide alternative

* From *A Free and Responsible Press,* the Report of the Commission on Freedom of the Press, ed. Robert Leigh. Copyright 1947 by The University of Chicago Press. Reprinted with permission of the publisher.

service where the drift toward monopoly seems dangerous.

3. Inquiries in areas where minority groups are excluded from reasonable access to the channels of communication.

4. Inquiries abroad regarding the picture of American life presented by the American press; and co-operation with agencies in other countries and with international agencies engaged in analysis of communication across national borders.

5. Investigation of instances of press lying, with particular reference to persistent misrepresentation of the data required for judging public issues.

6. Periodic appraisal of the tendencies and characteristics of the various branches of the communications industry.

7. Continuous appraisal of governmental action affecting communications.

8. Encouragement of the establishment of centers of advanced study, research, and criticism in the field of communications at universities.

9. Encouragement of projects which give hope of meeting the needs of special audiences.

10. The widest possible publicity and public discussion on all the foregoing.

The above recommendations taken together give some indication of methods by which the press may become accountable and hence remain free. We believe that if they are carried out, press performance will be brought much closer to the five ideal demands of society for the communication of news and ideas which were set forth in the second chapter: (1) a truthful, comprehensive, and intelligent account of the day's events in a context which gives them meaning; (2) a forum for the exchange of comment and criticism; (3) the projection of a representative picture of the constituent groups in the society; (4) the presentation and clarification of the goals and values of the society; (5) full access to the day's intelligence.

REPORT OF THE TASK FORCE
FOR A NATIONAL NEWS COUNCIL *

The United States is now passing through an era marked by divisive, often bitter, social conflict. New groups have coalesced to assault the privileges of the established; new ideas have arisen to challenge the validity of the old. Stridency and partisanship, militancy and defiance are in the air.

Reporting the news has always meant telling people things they may not want to hear. In times of social conflict, this task is all the more difficult. Skepticism turns to cynicism. Detachment is too often perceived as hostility. The clamor to "tell it like it is" too often carries with it the threat to "tell it like we see it, or else." The Greeks were not alone in wanting to condemn the bearer of bad tidings.

Disaffection with existing institutions, prevalent in every sector of society, has spread to the media of public information—newspapers and magazines, radio and television. Their accuracy, fairness, and responsibility have come under challenge. The media have found their credibility questioned, their freedom threatened, by public officials whose own credibility depends on the very media they attack and by citizens whose own freedom depends on the very institutions they threaten.

A free society cannot endure without a free press, and the freedom of the press ultimately rests on public understanding of, and trust in, its work.

The public as well as the press has a vital interest in enhancing the credibility of the media and in protecting their freedom of expression. One barrier to credibility is the absence in this country of any established national and

* From *A Free and Responsive Press*: The Twentieth Century Fund Task Force Report for a National News Council. © 1973 by The Twentieth Century Fund, New York.

independent mechanism for hearing complaints about the media or for examining issues concerning freedom of the press. Accordingly, this Task Force proposes:

That an independent and private national news council be established to receive, to examine, and to report on complaints concerning the accuracy and fairness of news reporting in the United States, as well as to initiate studies and report on issues involving the freedom of the press. The council shall limit its investigations to the principal national suppliers of news—the major wire services, the largest "supplemental" news services, the national weekly news magazines (including Life*), national newspaper syndicates, national daily newspapers, and the nationwide broadcasting networks.*

As a result of economic changes and technological advances, these few giant news organizations, with their unprecedented news gathering resources, now provide the majority of Americans with most of their national and international news. The Associated Press and United Press International, the two principal wire services, supply material to 99 percent of all daily newspapers as well as to most radio and television stations. Complementing these facilities are the major nationwide radio-television networks, the national weekly news magazines, national newspaper syndicates, nationwide daily newspapers (the *Wall Street Journal* and the *Christian Science Monitor*), and the "supplemental" news services, increasingly comprehensive wire services sold to large and small newspapers by organizations such as the *New York Times* and, jointly, the *Washington Post* and the *Los Angeles Times.*

This concentration of nationwide news organizations—like other large institutions—has grown increasingly remote from and unresponsive to the popular constituencies on which they depend and which depend on them. The national media council proposed by this Task Force will serve its purpose most effectively by focusing on the major national suppliers.

Publishers and broadcasters are justifiably suspicious of

any proposal—no matter how well intended—that might
compromise editorial independence, appear to substitute an
outsider's judgment for that of responsible editors, ensnare
newsmen in time-consuming explanations, or lend itself to
the long-term undermining of press freedom. The press of
the United States is among the best in the world and still
improving, but it fails to meet some of the standards of its
critics, among them, journalists. Moreover, a democratic
society has a legitimate and fundamental interest in the
quality of information available to it. Until now, the citizen
who was without benefit of special office, organization, or
resources had no place to bring his complaints. Until now,
neither the public nor the national news media have been
able to obtain detached and independent appraisals when
fairness and representativeness were questioned. The
proposed council is intended to provide this recourse for
both the public and the media.

The Council is not a panacea for the ills of the press or a
court weighing complaints about the responsibility of the
press. With its limited scope and lack of coercive power, the
Council will merely provide an independent forum for public
and press discussion of important issues affecting the flow of
information.

Editors and publishers may fear that a media council will
stimulate public hostility; some even suspect that it might
curtail rather than preserve their freedom. The core of the
media council idea, however, is the effort to make press
freedom more secure by providing an independent forum for
debate about media responsibility and performance, so that
such debate need not take place in government hearing
rooms or on the political campaign trail. The Task Force
unanimously believes that government should not be
involved in the evaluation of press practices. The Task Force
also recognizes that there is concern about the relationship
of press council procedures to the confidentiality of news
sources. It is convinced that the founders must address
themselves to the issue of confidentiality in the charter and
the Council must respect and uphold essential First
Amendment rights by maintaining confidentiality of news

sources and of material gathered in news production in its proceedings.*

The idea of a national council is not new. Sweden and Great Britain have had press councils for many years and one recently was set up in New Zealand. Britain's council, composed of private citizens and journalists, most closely resembles what the Task Force proposes.† Although the British council has not achieved all of its objectives in the past decade it has won substantial acceptance.

In the United States, a number of communities and one state—Minnesota—have in recent years established press councils. Some are no longer active; all appear to have been constructive regardless of their longevity, and experience has brought increasing accomplishment and decreasing mortality.

Significantly, the most recent and ambitious undertaking, Minnesota's, was initiated by a newspaper

* Hereafter asterisk indicates point on which Richard Salant abstains.

† Immediately after World War II, Britain was shaken by political and social dissonance similar to that of the United States today. Press mergers, closings, and allegations of sensationalism and slanting of news generated public concern and debate in and out of Parliament. The result of this debate was a Royal Commission investigation. The report of the commission recommended, among other measures, the creation of a private press council, to hear and act on complaints about the press and to speak in defense of press freedom when appropriate. Broadcasting (then only the government-sponsored BBC) was excluded from the recommendation.

Newspaper proprietors deliberated at length and delayed action for months; then agreed to a council with no public members. In 1963, after further Parliamentary threats and another Royal Commission report, the present successful citizen-journalist council was established.

Twenty of the Council's twenty-five members are chosen by eight publisher and journalistic staff organizations; the remaining five are public members elected for fixed terms by the Council. The chairman is also a public member. (Lord Devlin, one of Britain's most prominent judges, was the Council's first public chairman.) The secretariat is composed of three professional journalists. The Council's only power lies in the publicity given its findings. Its expenses—slightly more than $70,000 a year—are borne entirely by national press organizations.

"Foreigners who study the British Press Council usually come away in a mixed mood of admiration and bafflement," according to Vincent S. Jones, former executive editor of the Gannet Newspaper Editors. "It ought not to work, they feel, but somehow it does."

association. This development suggests that, as in Britain, opposition may be converted to neutrality and even support, as experience and objective observation dispel myths about the aims and operations of press councils.

Although the American Society of Newspaper Editors and other associations have failed to implement proposals for journalistic "ethics" or "grievance" machinery, investigations by this Task Force indicate that a substantial number of editors, publishers, and broadcasters will participate in a council experiment. As an editorial in the November 28, 1970, issue of *Editor and Publisher* observed: "Newspaper editors and publishers will never stand in the way of organizing such councils, but very few of them will be prime movers in setting them up."

The most frequently advanced proposal—a comprehensive nationwide press council on the British model—is impractical, if not undesirable, in the United States. The vastness and regional diversity of the United States, the number of individual publications and broadcasting stations, and problems of logistics and expense all militate against the formation of a comprehensive nationwide council. The weighing of one journalistic practice in New England against another in Arizona would present an impossible task. Nevertheless, individual newspapers and radio-television stations may find it useful to participate in regional, state, or local councils that are either now in existence or yet to be formed. This Task Force encourages the establishment of such councils. Several authorities have suggested that if such a comprehensive council eventually is formed, it will most likely evolve "from the ground up," possibly as a federation of local or regional councils. We urge that such councils be formed.

Accordingly, the Task Force makes the following recommendations for the establishment of a national council:

1. The body shall be called the Council on Press Responsibility and Press Freedom.
2. The Council's function shall be to receive, to examine, and to report on complaints concerning the accuracy and

fairness of news coverage in the United States as well as to study and to report on issues involving freedom of the press. The Council shall limit its review to news reporting by the principal national suppliers of news. Specifically identified editorial comment is excluded.

3. The principal national suppliers of news shall be defined as the nationwide wire services, the major "supplemental" wire services, the national weekly news magazines, national newspaper syndicates, national daily newspapers, nationwide commercial and noncommercial broadcast networks.

4. The Council shall consist of fifteen members, drawn from both the public and the journalism profession, but always with a public chairman. Both print and broadcast media shall be represented. No member shall be affiliated with the principal nationwide suppliers of news.*

5. A grievance committee, a subcommittee of the Council, will meet between eight and twelve times a year to screen public complaints. When appropriate, the committee and Council staff will engage teams of experts to investigate complaints.

6. The Council shall meet regularly and at such special meetings as shall be required. Its findings shall be released to the public in reports and press releases. Routine activities will be handled by a permanent staff, consisting of an Executive Director and professional assistants. The Executive Director should have significant journalistic experience.

7. Complaints about coverage by the designated national suppliers of news shall be handled according to procedures similar to those of the British and Minnesota press councils. Thus, the procedures will include a requirement that any complainant try to resolve his grievance with the media organization involved before the Council may initiate action on a complaint. Complainants will be required to waive the right to legal proceedings in court on any matter taken up in Council proceedings.

It is expected that most complaints will be settled without recourse to formal Council action.*

8. Individuals and organizations may bring complaints to the Council. The Council may initiate inquiry into any

situation where governmental action threatens freedom of the press.

9. Action by the Council will be limited to the public reporting of Council decisions. The Council will have no enforcement powers.

10. Where extensive field investigation is required, the Council may appoint fact-finding task forces.

11. The Council's executive offices shall be at a location designated by its members. Regardless of the ultimate location, the Council shall consider emphasizing its national character by scheduling at least some meetings on a rotating basis throughout the country.

12. The Task Force shall appoint a founding committee which will select the Council's original members, incorporate the Council, adopt its constitution, and establish the initial budget.

13. Terms of office shall be three years (with terms of charter members to be staggered on the basis of a drawing of lots); members shall be limited to two consecutive terms. Members must resign from the Council if they leave the vocational category which was the basis for their selection. On retirement of a Council member, the Council shall appoint a nominating committee made up of representatives from foundations, the media, and the public. The Council shall make the final selection from the choices presented to it.

14. The founding committee shall incorporate the Council and establish the initial budget for a minimum of three to six years. It is suggested that the annual budget will be approximately $400,000.*

15. The Task Force appoints Justice Roger Traynor, former chief justice of California, head of the founding committee and chairman of the Council.

16. The Council's processes, findings, and conclusions should not be employed by government agencies, specifically the Federal Communications Commission, in its decisions on broadcast license renewals. Failure to observe this recommendation would discourage broadcasters from supporting or cooperating with the Council.

The national media council proposed here will not resolve all the problems facing the print and broadcast media, nor will it answer all of the criticisms voiced by the public and by the politicians. It will, however, be an independent body to which the public can take its complaints about press coverage. It will act as a strong defender of press freedom. It will attempt to make the media accountable to the public and to lessen the tensions between the press and the government.

Any independent mechanism that might contribute to better public understanding of the media and that will foster accurate and fair reporting and public accountability of the press must not be discouraged or ignored. The national media council is one such mechanism that must be established now.

Appendix C
PRESS COUNCIL
OPERATING RULES

This appendix includes the operating rules and
Constitution of the Minnesota Press Council, approved in
1971. They were revised in March 1974 as this book went to
press.

CONSTITUTION OF THE
MINNESOTA PRESS COUNCIL

I. *Title.* The Minnesota Press Council, hereinafter called the
Council, is a voluntary extra-legal body constituted on and
from February 19, 1971.

II. *Purpose.* The purpose of the Council is: (A) to preserve the
freedom of the press; (B) to maintain the character of the

press in accordance with the highest professional standards; (C) to consider complaints about the conduct of the Minnesota press, including advertising, as well as the conduct of persons and organizations towards the Minnesota press, and to deal with these complaints in whatever manner is reasonably practical and appropriate; (D) to review, on a continuing basis, the performance of the Minnesota press regarding matters of general public interest; and (E) to urge and assist the Minnesota press in the fulfillment of its unique responsibility to perform in the public interest.

III. *Membership.*

   A. The Council shall consist of eighteen members selected from the following groups:
      1. Nine of the members shall be selected from the general Minnesota public at large.
      2. Nine of the members shall be selected from members of the Minnesota press. At least two of these members shall be non-management and non-ownership members of the press.

   B. New members on the Council shall be selected by members on the Council. Such members shall be selected in equal proportions to their representation on the Council as provided in paragraph B of this Article III.
      The total membership on the Council may be increased to a maximum of twenty-four members. If additional members are added to the Council, they shall be selected in equal proportions to their representation on the Council as provided for in paragraph A of this Article III. A decision to increase the membership on the Council shall require the approval of the two-thirds majority of the members present and voting at a meeting, which two-thirds majority shall not be less than a simple majority of the membership of the Council. No decision to increase the membership on the Council shall be effective unless at least twenty-eight days' notice of

such proposed action shall have been given in writing to all Council members.

C. Upon nomination to the Council, a person shall be entitled to membership for three consecutive years. At the end of this period the member, if he or she is qualified, shall be eligible for reappointment. Upon first appointment of the group of members specified in paragraph A of this Article III, six shall serve for only one year before retirement and a further six for an initial period of two years. These members shall be decided by lot. They will be eligible for reappointment, and thereafter the normal period of their membership on the Council and that of their successors shall be three years.

D. Any member of the Council ceasing to be qualified as a member of the Minnesota press or as a non-management or non-ownership member of the Minnesota press shall notify the Secretary of the Council within one calendar month of the change in his, or her, status, and his, or her, membership shall thereafter terminate within three calendar months. A person filling such a vacancy, or any vacancy on the Council, shall be appointed to membership in like manner to that by which the person whose vacancy he, or she, fills was appointed. Upon initial appointments he, or she, shall retain membership only for the expired portion of the period which remained to the person whose place on the Council he, or she, takes.

IV. *Officers.* At the first meeting of the calendar year, the Council shall elect from its membership a President, a Vice-President, and a Treasurer, who shall serve terms of one year. The Council shall also elect a Secretary, who need not be a member of the Council, and who shall serve at the pleasure of the Council.

The President shall be the presiding officer at the meetings of the Council. He shall be the spokesman for the Council. He shall, with the approval of the Council, appoint committees and subcommittees to report to the Council. He shall cause to be distributed a summary of each meeting to the members of the Council.

The Vice-President shall preside at all meetings when the President is not in attendance and shall automatically assume the presidency whenever a President resigns or for any reason ceases to be an active member of the Council.

The Secretary shall perform the usual duties of a Secretary, including but not limited to, sending out notices of all meetings and recording and preserving the minutes of all meetings. The Secretary, at the direction of the President and the chairman of the Grievance Committee, shall also investigate such matters and complaints as the Council shall, from time to time, deem necessary.

The Treasurer shall be responsible for establishing a procedure for the collection of dues and contributions, and accounting for all receipts and disbursements at each annual meeting. The Treasurer shall be bonded in an amount approved by the Council. He may, with the consent of the Council, appoint a deputy who also shall be bonded in the same way.

Should a vacancy occur in the office of the Secretary or of the Treasurer, successors shall be elected by the Council.

V. *Quorum.* A quorum at the Council meeting shall be one-half of the voting members of the Council plus one member.

VI. *Committees.* The President shall, with the approval of the Council, appoint committees of its members for the discharge of such duties as the Council shall from time to time specify.

VII. *Procedures.* Each member of the Council shall be entitled to cast one vote in any matter decided by them on a show of hands or by ballot. All parties to a grievance shall have the opportunity to appear in person before an appropriate Council body considering the grievance to give evidence and present testimony.

The Council shall have no direct or coercive powers. Its actions shall be limited to the issuance of public statements expressing the Council's views.

VIII. *Finances.* Funds for the operations of the Council may be obtained by dues and contributions.

IX. *Amendments or Repealers.* Amendments to or repealers of any Articles of the Constitution shall require the approval of a two-thirds majority of the members present and voting at a meeting, which two-thirds majority shall not be less than a simple majority of the membership of the Council. No amendment or repealer shall be effective unless at least twenty-eight days' notice of a proposed amendment or repealer shall have been given in writing to all Council members.

X. *Dissolution.* The Council may at any time terminate its existence. A resolution to dissolve the Council, to be binding, must be passed by a two-thirds majority of its members present and voting at a meeting specially called for that purpose, which two-thirds majority shall be not less than a simple majority of the membership of the Council. Not less than twenty-eight days' notice shall be given of any such meeting and such notice shall give particulars of the purpose for which the meeting is called. Upon dissolution all remaining unencumbered funds shall be contributed to the University of Minnesota to be used for scholarships in its School of Journalism and Mass Communication.

Grievance Committee Procedural Rules, Minnesota Press Council (1971)

One of the primary functions of the Minnesota Press Council is consideration and processing of grievances against the Press and the editors and employees of the Press. The Council will undertake to hear, consider and adjust grievances after determining the essential facts of any controversy through hearings and any necessary investigations. In order to function effectively and fairly it is essential that a separate Grievance Committee be created and that operating procedures be established for the Committee. While a complete set of procedural rules must be provided for those instances where proper consideration of the grievance will require application of a full range of procedural rules, it is expected that the vast majority of grievances will not require such formal handling. For example, while due process rights such as the right of counsel are provided, it is expected that the parties will seek to have their attorneys directly involved only on very rare occasions in the processing of a grievance. The nature of the Council's function is such that informality of the proceedings is beneficial and formality at every stage will be discouraged.

While the composition of the Grievance Committee is not properly a subject for inclusion in these procedural rules, these rules are based upon the expectation that the Grievance Committee will be structured to directly reflect the same composition of public and professional interests as are reflected in the membership of the Press Council.

As used in these procedural rules the following terms shall be considered technical terms and to have the following meaning:

Press. Newspapers of general circulation in the state of Minnesota

Newspaper. The particular newspaper against whom a complaint or grievance has been made

Complainant. A person or organization who has or makes a grievance against a newspaper

I. Instituting or Commencing Grievances

    A. Exhaustion of local remedies. No grievance should be processed unless the matter has first been presented to the newspaper by the complainant.

        Comment. The purpose of the Press Council is primarily to encourage mutual understanding between the Press and the local citizenry. One of the simplest and most effective methods to insure mutual understanding is personal face to face discussion of problem areas and disputes among the persons involved. The discussion should involve the editor or publisher of the newspaper and the complainant directly. By this personal meeting imagined affronts and misunderstandings can often be cleared up. If personal discussion with the local editor is made first, it will give the editor an opportunity to understand the nature and extent of the complainant's concern, to be advised more clearly regarding matters that are occurring in his community, and to more precisely present the newspaper's position. If the newspaper agrees it is in error, it will be possible for immediate corrective action to be taken by the newspaper, including publishing corrections. If the matter is not an error of the newspaper, but arises through misunderstanding by the complainant of the function of the Press, perhaps discussion of professional standards and understanding of the problems of the Press will resolve the problem at that point. If nothing else, at least the parties will be introduced to each other and the areas of dispute acknowledged and recognized between them.

Each grievance shall be temporarily withheld from further processing until the grievance has been presented to the newspaper and the newspaper has been given an opportunity to discuss the matter with the complainant and for such time as may be reasonably necessary for the parties to take such corrective actions as either party may deem desirable.

B. Grievances can be brought by individuals and private and public entities against a newspaper, but not against individual employees of the newspaper.

Comment. The newspaper should be considered responsible for the conduct of all of its employees in terms of the newspaper's relationship to the public. Therefore the grievance should be directed against the newspaper even though the actual cause may arise from conduct by an individual editor, reporter, or other employee.

In those grievances where it appears that a reporter's or other employee's professional conduct is the primary source of the grievance, the reporter or employee involved should be personally informed of the grievance and given an opportunity to participate directly in the proceeding as though he were in fact a party to the proceeding. In no event, however, will the newspaper be relieved of its ultimate responsibility for the conduct of its employees or be permitted to have the grievance dropped as to it. At all times it must be recognized that it is the complainant's grievance that is the sole issue before the Grievance Committee.

C. No grievance will be considered if legal action based on the same subject matter is pending against the newspaper or an individual journalist. A grievance will not be processed until the complainant waives any possible future civil action that he may have arising out of the grievance for matters occurring prior to the filing of the grievance.

Comment. It would seem desirable for the Council not to be involved in grievances in which litigation is pending. In like measure, it would not be desirable for the Council to consider a matter when the same or related matter may ultimately be presented to a court as a part of a civil claim. If a complainant wishes to invoke the process of the Press Council, he should recognize his resort to the Press Council will be his exclusive remedy for all matters relating to the subject matter of the grievance. Waivers of civil actions, of course, should not be waivers of legal actions for future incidents of alleged misconduct or repetition of the matter involved in the pending complaint.

D. A party filing a grievance should waive libel and slander claims against persons providing the Council with information, against members of the Council and against the Press for publication of information acquired by the Council during its investigation and hearing process, or included in the Council's report.

Comment. Proceedings by the Press Council are not protected by statutory privilege. As such, the Council should undertake to provide protection to persons giving information to the Press Council and protection to members of the Council to encourage high level professional and citizen involvement in the Council activities. Waivers of libel and slander claims contribute some incentive for full and complete participation both by the public, Council members, and the Press.

E. Grievances resolved by agreement between the

complainant and the newspaper following its
presentation to the newspaper should not be further
processed and the matter should be dropped at that
point. No formal record should be kept of the
grievance thus resolved.

> *Comment.* If the matter is disposed of following the initial
> presentation of the grievance to the newspaper, it would
> seem that the adjustment is personal and between the
> parties. The Press Council should not review the
> adjustment or indicate any assent or dissent to the
> arrangement. Since no responsibility is taken for the
> action, a record should not be maintained for the details of
> the initial inquiry other than the fact that it has been
> disposed of by personal adjustment.

F. Grievances to be further considered by the Council
must be filed with the Council in written form.

> *Comment.* If the complainant has difficulty expressing his
> grievance in written form, members of the Council staff
> should be free to assist the complainant in this endeavor.
> Care should be taken by the staff to insure that the facts
> are accurately expressed and that the staff person does not
> improperly influence or suggest additional areas of
> concern to the complainant.

II. Grievance Processing

A. Upon receipt of a written grievance, a copy of the
grievance must be sent to the newspaper with a
request that the newspaper reply promptly to the
grievance in writing setting forth the newspaper's
contentions.

> *Comment.* Procedurally it is desirable that each party's
> formal position be reflected by written statements. Since a
> written grievance initiates the process, it would seem
> desirable to have the newspaper's response also in written
> form. By compelling a writing at an early stage, the parties
> are less free to change positions factually later on in the
> proceedings, but more importantly, the parties are forced
> to think through their positions more clearly. There is no
> prejudice to the newspaper if the newspaper refuses to
> cooperate with the Council at this stage and refuses to
> provide a written statement. The opportunity to make a
> statement is a privilege, not an obligation. A failure to

respond does not indicate agreement with the facts asserted in the grievance. A right to participate personally in future hearings can be denied until a written response is made.

B. The Grievance Committee will review each filed grievance. The committee may establish and adopt a procedure for processing grievances, including a method for a preliminary screening of grievances.

Comment. The Grievance Committee should be responsible for determining the sufficiency of each filed grievance and for adopting its own policies with regard to the method of processing grievances best designed to insure proper processing. The Committee should be free to adopt a preliminary screening procedure if it desires. In like measure, the Committee should have the freedom to determine whether or not each grievance must be processed by the entire Committee as a preliminary matter. Once the Committee has experience in processing grievances, the Committee should be free to amend its internal procedures without the necessity of obtaining approval from the entire Press Council and requiring an amendment to these procedural rules.

C. The Grievance Committee shall make a preliminary and informal fact investigation including discussions with the complainant, the newspaper, the newspaper's reporters or employees, and witnesses. The investigation may be conducted by a designated staff person or members of the Committee and can involve written communication as well as personal conferences or telephone communication.

Comment. Preliminary informal fact investigation is desirable to verify the facts alleged in the grievance and in the response. The Committee should be free to adopt whatever method is most desirable in a particular case or type of case for determining accuracy of statements and resolving questions regarding the nature of the grievance. No formal investigation steps should be required other than those steps the Committee deems necessary to determine whether or not a grievance is factually meritorious.

D. If the grievance should be dismissed after preliminary

investigation, the Grievance Committee should so advise the Press Council and, if concurred in by the Press Council, copies of the dismissal will be transmitted in written form to the complainant and to the newspaper together with a brief statement explaining the reasons for the dismissal.

E. A record will be kept of all grievances and the disposition of the grievance, including letters of dismissals. A summary of the record will be sent to all Council members periodically for their information.

F. If the Grievance Committee decides further Committee action is necessary, a hearing time will be scheduled for the Committee to consider the evidence and hear witnesses presented by the parties. All parties will have the opportunity to appear in person before the Committee and give oral testimony. Non-party witnesses can be called and examined only in the discretion of the Committee. A right to cross examination and a right to counsel are available for both parties. Normally no transcript of the hearing will be made, but the Committee or any party shall have the privilege of preserving the evidence in any reasonable manner he chooses, such as the use of tape recordings, etc. At all times the desirability of informality and flexibility of the proceedings must be recognized.

Comment. A hearing may be necessary for the Committee to get a true flavor of the dispute and to determine the credibility of persons giving evidence by observing their demeanor. Basic due process requirements of confrontation, cross-examination and counsel should be available if the parties desire to exercise those rights, but such use should be discouraged and should be the exception, not the rule. The British believe that this type of administrative proceedings should not involve due process procedural protection. In this country it is generally believed that better factual results will be obtained if due process requirements are available for those rare situations where they are needed, or for persons who would feel more comfortable if assisted by an attorney, or for persons who want to examine an adverse witness.

G. Additional investigations can be made and additional evidence can be presented to the Committee after the hearing at the direction of the Committee.

> *Comment.* At the end of the hearing questions may still exist with regard to fact matters. The Committee should be able to obtain this information either by investigation or by additional hearings.

H. The Grievance Committee by majority vote will make the Committee's decision on the matter and recommend corrective action if any is deemed desirable. If a grievance involves a matter of broad general policy or could involve more than the one newspaper grieved against, the grievance must be transmitted to the Press Council for deliberation with or without recommendation by the Grievance Committee.

> *Comment.* Certain grievances may involve matters of general policy that properly should be considered as policy questions by the entire Press Council. Such grievances must be considered and resolved by the Council, and the Grievance Committee is free to refer such a grievance to the Press Council at any stage of its proceeding whenever the Committee feels that such referral is proper.

III. Recommendations and Reports

A. Except for grievances involving matters of general policy covered under II, H, conclusions and recommendations of the Grievance Committee will be transmitted to each of the parties in writing. Each party will be given a period of ten days to submit responses to the recommendations in writing before consideration of the recommendations by the Press Council.

> *Comment.* It would seem desirable that each party be advised of the intended report before public release of the recommendations of the Grievance Committee. If errors are made factually or legally the parties will have an opportunity to correct such errors.

B. All recommendations of the Grievance Committee will be transmitted to the Press Council for its consideration.

> *Comment.* The recommendation of the Grievance Committee and the parties' response thereto should be sent to all members of the Press Council prior to the Council meeting.

C. The Press Council will consider the recommendation of the Grievance Committee, and by majority of the Press Council members voting on the question can accept, reject, or amend the recommendation, or it can return the grievance to the Committee for further processing. After final action by the Press Council, the Press Council will make a written report of its action.

D. The report of the Press Council will be transmitted to the parties and to the news media for publication.

IV. Appeal to the Council

A. Appeals from a dismissal by the Grievance Committee, or from a report of the Council in grievances where the parties have not previously appeared before the Council, will be permitted only at the discretion of the Press Council.

> *Comment.* An automatic appeal with an extended hearing by the entire Council in each case would not be beneficial in terms of preserving Grievance Committee integrity or in permitting the Council time to consider its other functions. Appeals involving new fact hearings should be the exception, not the rule. No party has a right to a new fact hearing or to appear personally before the entire Council. Such matters should be discretionary with the Press Council.

B. Such appeals to the Press Council, when granted, ordinarily shall not be hearings de novo, but in the discretion of the Council new evidence may be heard.

C. The Press Council's deliberations need not be public.

D. Following the Press Council's deliberations, its recommendations will be reported to each of the parties and to the Press in the form of a report and the report can be published.

Appendix D
CRITICAL ATTITUDES
TOWARD THE MEDIA

This appendix is limited to results published in a report by
Joe Lewels, Jr., then of the University of Missouri, and
originally published in a 1972 report (No. 281) of the
Freedom of Information Center of that university. It is
reprinted with permission of the author and the Freedom
of Information Center. It is of particular interest here
because it scientifically determines types of critics of the
press surprisingly similar to those described by T. S. Eliot
and discussed in chapter 1 of this book.

Lewels since has been appointed chairman of the
department of journalism, University of Texas at El Paso.

CRITICAL ATTITUDES TOWARD
THE MEDIA

The Procedure

Attitudes in this study were determined via Q-technique, a set of procedures developed by William Stephenson (1953) to study complex matters of human behavior—such as attitudes. Subjects operantly define their attitudes by sorting opinion statements according to their degree of agreement or disagreement. In Q, persons are factor analyzed across a sample of tests, resulting in clusters of persons (Q-factors) who have sorted the statements in similar, i.e., correlated, ways. A Q-factor represents a hypothetical person—a kind of composite individual whose makeup is composed of all those individuals who are part of the factor.

Subjects were asked to sort the 55 opinion statements along a forced-distribution 11-point continuum ranging from most agree to most disagree. Upon completion of the sorting, they were asked to comment on the three items they placed at each extreme end of the continuum.

The forty subjects who participated in the study were selected on the basis of their backgrounds with an effort to include persons with specific interests or involvement in the media. Because the study was designed to tap activist attitudes, no attempt was made to obtain a random sample of the total U.S. population. Instead, the object was to understand how those persons who are active in challenging the established press feel about the media as compared to how journalists feel. It was also felt that it would be valuable to include in the sample a group of people with no involvement or special interests.

The resulting sample consisted of forty persons categorized into five broad areas: print journalism; broadcast journalism; advertising, media challengers, and nonmedia.

Included in the sample were newsmen, broadcasters, publishers, journalism students, journalism professors, editors of journalism reviews, nonjournalists involved in community radio stations, members of citizen pressure groups, consumer advocates, blue-collar workers, elementary school teachers, clerical workers, and a few nonmedia professionals.

Opinion statements used in the study were selected from material on file with the Freedom of Information Center, from questionnaires completed by editors of journalism reviews, from personal interviews and from statements made pro and con to media during the recent Senate subcommittee hearings on freedom of the press conducted by Senator Sam Ervin. Statements fell into a number of broad categories such as news distortion, media responsibility, minority access, consumer issues, government regulation, etc.

Following are the results of the data analysis which provided a six-factor solution. In other words, after factor analysis, the subjects fell into six major categories or types.* The author's subjective interpretation of these categories follows.

Factor I: The Revolutionary

Perhaps because there was a special effort made to include in the sample people who were known to be highly critical of the media, the results show the largest factor to be comprised of individuals who might be classified as revolutionaries. This is not to say that they advocate overthrow of the media or of the government through violent means, but rather that they approximate closely the ideology that seems to inspire the so-called social revolution this country is going through.

It should be emphasized that even though this factor had by far the most people of all six factors (13), it cannot be generalized that this type is as strongly represented in the general American population.

This factor was defined by those involved in community broadcasting stations, those seeking access to the media, minority-group members, editors of journalism reviews, and some journalists. Statements that typify this attitude tend to

* A principle-axis-factor solution with varimax rotation.

fall into three major categories: minority rights, corporate tyranny, and media irresponsibility. The most highly ranked statement was "Freedom of the press, as expressed in the First Amendment, means freedom for every citizen to have access to the nation's media." Such a statement is a radical departure from the traditional American belief that freedom of the press is basically the freedom of the media owner to print what he chooses without interference from government or any other outside source. Indeed, the other five types either disagreed strongly with this view or treated it as a neutral item.

The high ranking of this statement also indicates that there may be a significant proportion of the population beginning to believe that free-press guarantees of the First Amendment do not solely apply to the press, but to the individual citizen as well.

The people on this factor place a high priority on the media's connection with big business and what they perceive as the powerful institutions that try to perpetuate the status quo. They feel that the "establishment" media cannot serve the public "because they are organized to serve the advertiser"; "because class bias permeates the media, resulting in a distorted reflection of reality"; and because "Rather than being an advocate for the underdog, the press is an advocate of nearly all the powerful institutions of the community."

The Revolutionary views censorship in quite a different way than would a traditional journalist:

A form of censorship already exists when the news is determined by a handful of men responsible only to their corporate employers and is filtered through a handful of commentators.

The emphasis on this type of statement implies that the Revolutionary is challenging the concept of "laissez faire" economics that he thinks has allowed big business to dominate the media. He believes that this is at least as great a threat to democracy and a free marketplace of ideas as government control of the media.

Statements rated negatively also illustrate this antagonism toward big business: "What is good for big business is good for the country," and, "If it were not for the advertising dollar, TV programing would be pathetic."

The end result of this pronounced antipathy toward the established press is a desire to provide a check-and-balance system to keep the media in line. Although direct censorship is completely ruled out ("No government agency should be set up to determine what is authentic or biased in news reporting") the Revolutionary believes that there must be government regulations ("Limited regulation of the media gives important minority views the right to be heard"). The idea of nongovernmental advisory boards (press councils) to act as a conscience for the media did not strongly appeal to this type, although it was positively ranked.

Despite the low esteem in which they hold the media, persons on factor I are concerned about the rights of newsmen and the function of the press as an investigator of government affairs.

Generally speaking, the Revolutionary would like to see some drastic changes in the media and their role in society. He holds high the First Amendment guaranatees of a free press, but would extend that guarantee to every citizen, not just the owners of the media. In order to guarantee this right, he is willing to have some government control of the press, if it will ensure that minority views will be presented.

Factor II: The Pro-Media Critic

Factor II individuals provide more moderate criticism of the media and show a greater concern for government infringement on the rights of the press. They believe that "the press is essentially doing a good job," and that "most of the criticism is unjust because there is no way to please everyone." The real dangers to a free press lie in government control. The most highly rated statement for type II was "The only thing that makes a democratic government safe is knowledge: facts about what is really going on in the government." They strongly believe that "No government agency should be set up to determine what is authentic or biased in news reporting," and that "The public interest demands that newsmen be protected from forcible disclosure of their sources." People on factor II were the only ones who generally agreed with the statement that "the mass media should be completely free."

This type is a defender of broadcasters' rights under the First Amendment and the right of the publisher to print or not to print whatever he wishes. The statement ranked highest by the Revolutionary: "Freedom of the press as expressed in the First Amendment means freedom for every citizen to have access to the nation's media," was ranked highly negative by the type II individual. Much more realistic than the idealistic Revolutionary, the Pro-Media Critic believes that "People actually project their own political biases on the media." They also believe that it would be unrealistic to allow free access to everyone. Comments on the subject of access indicated that type II individuals see a need for the exercise of news judgment by those in the media, rather than allowing the government to decide which views represent a true minority.

Despite the consistency of pro-media views, type II criticizes the press for not assuming enough social responsibility, and for not providing enough interpretive reporting. The Pro-Media Critic sees the media as being too sensitive: "They call it free speech when they attack the government, but when government snaps back it's called intimidation." This indicates that even though the government is seen as a real threat, this group believes that a press-government adversary role is a healthy relationship.

Absent from this type's attitude toward the media is the concern for minority views that typified the Revolutionary attitude and a lack of concern about the dangers of the media being dominated by big business. Although this group reacted negatively to the statement "What's good for big business is good for the country," their reaction was much less negative than that of type I. They also disagreed that the media "cannot serve the public because they are organized to serve the advertiser." Statements ranked most negatively were those that were overcritical of the media:

American youth is being morally corrupted by the bombardment of smut in all media.

The most powerful of the nation's media are owned by a small group of eastern intellectuals who band together to determine what is or is not to be considered news.

Much of what is aired on TV news is disturbing, depressing, and ugly. It usually doesn't reflect the world as it really is.

The media are not being socially responsible when they publish secret government documents.

Generally, the Pro-Media Critic sees the press as a vital force in maintaining a democracy and would like to see the media as free of government control as possible. Their criticisms are directed at the failures of the media to provide enough consumer information and enough interpetive analysis of news events. Significantly, the six people on this factor all have some connection with journalism and all have at least a college education. One is a professor of journalism and the rest are graduate students in journalism.

Again, the key to understanding the attitude of this factor lies in the definition of freedom of the press. This type is a firm believer in the traditional role of the press in a capitalistic society. They see little wrong with the media operating as a private enterprise and support the rights of the media owners to operate independently of outside interference. Yet, they can see many ways to improve the media from within. The Pro-Media Critic would be in favor of self-regulatory methods of improvement and can see little need for even nongovernmental advisory boards to act as a conscience for the media.

Factor III: The Silent Majority

Although small in size (four people) factor III is worth interpreting because of its uniqueness. It is interesting that all those who fall on factor III have quite similar backgrounds. All have little more than a high school education, and all come from small midwestern communities. Two are clerical workers, one is a blue-collar worker, and the fourth is a housewife. Consistent in their attitudes is a general criticism of the media and a support of big business and free enterprise.

The Silent Majority believes that there is too much interpretation and analysis of news by the media. They believe that the news "should be presented as objectively as possible so that people can interpret it for themselves." They agree strongly with the statement that "The press today seems paranoid. They call it free speech when they attack the government, but when government snaps back it's called intimidation." Significantly, this is the only group that agreed with the statement that is most progovernment: "The media are not being socially responsible in my view when they publish secret government documents."

This type of criticism suggests the lack of support that the media have among the general public. The type III individual is likely to be politically conservative and sees the media as a liberal force. The Silent Majority believes that "Broadcast journalists tend to be biased against those who are politically conservative," and deny vehemently that "The political commitment of the mass media has always been and still is decidedly Republican." To them, the media tend to lean to the left and need some kind of restrictions placed upon them. The Silent Majority type rated the statement "The mass media should be completely free," strongly negative. Despite this attitude, it could be of some comfort to those in the media to know that even the Silent Majority believes that there should be "no government agency set up to determine what is authentic or biased in news reporting." They also believe that "The only thing that makes a democratic government safe is knowledge: facts about what is really going on in the government." Also reassuring for the press is the fact that this group disagreed with the famous Agnew statement about the media being owned by "eastern intellectuals who band together to determine what is or is not to be considered news."

Although the type III individual criticizes the media for not having enough "good consumer information" in advertising, he is the only one who agreed with the statement that supports the commercial nature of the media: "Advertisers have a right to expect pleased audiences, not audiences that may turn some of their displeasure about the program toward the sponsor's product." The Silent Majority believes that "Corporations, including media, should assume more responsibility for what they do," yet does not see the corporate structure of our economy as a particularly threatening force. This group ranked the statement "The tyranny of the corporate conglomerate is as dangerous as the tyranny of government," in the neutral category.

Areas in which this type would like to see the media regulated include the preservation of law and order and the national security ("The government should be able to force the media to divulge its sources of information . . ."); the area of consumer information ("Ads don't have enough good consumer information for people to make wise buying decisions"); newspaper monopoly ("I don't like newspaper monopoly, it's a good thing to have a couple of papers to choose from that are competing against each other"); and minority access ("Limited regulation of the media gives important minority views the right to be heard . . .").

Yet, even though they are for limited access for minority views, the Silent Majority is wary of minority activist groups: "The clamor for access to the media has brought out all the vultures who are trying to get something for nothing from those who have worked hard for what they have," and, "Although there is nothing basically wrong with pressure groups conveying their ideas and recommendations to the media, their tactics are often reprehensible." They see the move for minority access as a social detriment: "There has developed a dangerous movement for the purpose of coercing the media to accept the viewpoints of minority groups."

It can be summarized that the Silent Majority is distrustful of the media's liberal tendencies and, although they rely on the media as a watchdog over government, they would not grant the press any absolute freedoms that would endanger the American system. They are not very tolerant of minority groups seeking access to the media or of radical views that find their way into the press. They do not see any great danger in the private-enterprise nature of the media even though they strongly agree that "corporations, including media, must assume more responsibility for what they do."

Factor IV: The Critical Intellectual

The Critical Intellectual has little or no involvement in the world of journalism but is intellectually attuned to the problems of the journalist and the role of the press as a watchdog over government. From his ivory tower, he can see the press as a fighter for the underdog and as a force that in most cases will uncover and expose the truth wherever it may lie. However, he is concerned about the monopolistic tendencies of the media and of corporations in general and believes in regulating big business to keep it in line with needs of society. He is particularly concerned with the difficulties of getting minority views into the media and considers this issue an important one for a democratic country.

The minimum education for the five persons on factor IV was a college degree, with one holding a Master of Science degree and another holding a Doctor of Philosophy degree.

Similar to the Pro-Media Critic, the Critical Intellectual is concerned with too much government interference in the flow of news and with the role of the press as a seeker of truth about government. The most highly ranked statement for this type was: "The only thing that makes a democratic government safe is knowledge: facts about what is really going on in the government." He would also agree that "No government agency should be set up to determine what is authentic or biased in news reporting," and he strongly believes that the press has the right to print secret government documents, if it is in the public interest.

He too believes in the right of the publisher to print or

not to print whatever he chooses, and he thinks that threatening to take the license away from a broadcaster is too severe a regulation. Both of these statements were ranked high by factor IV:

> Even as freedom of the press implies the freedom to be heard, we must not forget that it also implies the freedom to print or not to print. This is a freedom for the publisher.

> The ultimate intimidation is to threaten to attempt to take a broadcast license away from its owners. This goes against our tradition of a free enterprise system.

Like the Pro-Media Critic, he is against newspaper monopoly and is critical of advertising for not having enough good consumer information and of the press for not giving enough coverage to consumer issues.

But here the similarity ends. The Critical Intellectual tends to agree with the Revolutionary's interpretation of the First Amendment: "Freedom of the press, as expressed in the First Amendment means freedom for every citizen to have access to the nation's media," a statement that the Pro-Media Critic and the Silent Majority are strongly against. In fact, the Critical Intellectual is a firm believer in the rights of minorities.

The third most negatively ranked statement for this group was: "Forcing minority opinions into a newspaper would be very harmful to the social good. It would epitomize social irresponsibility." This indicates that people on factor IV would be in favor of some government regulation of the media to ensure access to minority views.

The second most negatively ranked statement, "There should be no limitation to the number of newspapers or television stations a person can own," is another indication of the belief that the government must have a hand in regulating the media.

Indeed, the statement "Once the government gets its foot in the door, even a little bit, government regulation will grow. Eventually, we will have a press that is controlled by government," was rated strongly negative. And one of the respondents on this factor commented that "the media have demonstrated that they will not police themselves; we have to have some government controls." He qualified this remark by saying that "there is a fine line between control and censor!"

Another way in which the Critical Intellectual's attitude toward the media differs from the Pro-Media Critic and the Silent Majority is in his fear of corporate control and power. The third most positively ranked statement, "Corporations, including media, must assume more responsibility for what they do," shows a high concern for corporate responsibility. Significantly, the Critical Intellectual agreed with the Revolutionary in his assessment of corporate dangers in the media: "A form of censorship already exists when the news is determined by a handful of men responsible only to their corporate employers and is filtered through a handful of commentators." All other factors rated this statement completely neutral, and it is a key statement in understanding the Critical Intellectual's media philosophy.

Despite his support of the media in most areas, the Critical Intellectual is wary of the way news is presented. He believes that "There is too much interpretation and analysis of news by the media. It should be presented as objectively as possible so that people can interpret it for themselves." He is also aware of the human failings of those in the media: "A reporter may be ordered to be objective, but he knows how his paper or station wants stories presented."

In summary, the Critical Intellectual is one who is liberal in his views on civil rights and the rights of the media to act free of government control, yet he is in favor of government regulation that is necessary to balance the power of the "establishment" press with the rights of the public. Keeping channels of communication open is of utmost importance to the Critical Intellectual.

Factor V: The Traditional Journalist

Factor V is composed of five persons who have had extensive experience in the media as journalists, particularly in newspaper work. One is an award-winning reporter and currently a professor of journalist, two are publishers of newspapers and one is a former newspaper publisher and editor who is now teaching journalism. As might be expected from the composition of this group, there is a heavy leaning toward the rights of the print media with less concern for broadcasting's role in American journalism. As is implied by the name, the Traditional Journalist feels compelled to defend the media from undue criticism, yet his liberal journalist values are evident.

Not surprisingly, the statement most strongly agreed with was: "I tend to find newspapers more believable than broadcast news." One of the respondents commented that in his opinion, "newspapers separate news and opinion; television does not."

This group rated the statement "Even as freedom of the press implies the freedom to be heard, we must not forget that it also implies the freedom to print or not to print. This is a freedom for the publisher," more positively than any other type. Yet the Traditional Journalist believes that "broadcast journalists tend to be biased against those who are politically conservative," and denies that "The broadcasting system in the U.S. would be substantially destroyed or eroded if broadcasters are not provided with government protection from citizen pressure groups." However, he does stand up for his broadcast counterpart by disagreeing most strongly with a derogatory statement about broadcasting: "The history of broadcasting in the U.S. is littered with the bodies of those who wanted to do something significant and who were driven out by the pimps and thieves who now run the media." This statement, one respondent comments, "is irresponsible name calling."

This type is greatly concerned with the rights of the press in a free society. The second most highly ranked statement was: "No government agency should be set up to determine what is authentic or biased in news reporting." Other statements defending the media were also ranked highly:

> The public interest demands that newsmen be protected from forcible disclosure of their sources.

> As long as there is competition between media and their newsmen, it is unlikely that any one publisher or broadcaster could forever suppress the news.

> People actually project their own political biases on the news media. The extreme right sees the media as a communist conspiracy and the extreme left sees the media as members of the establishment.

> The media are essentially doing a good job. Most of the criticism is unjust because there is no way to please everyone.

The Traditional Journalist had a strong negative reaction to the following antimedia statements:

> American youth is being morally corrupted by the bombardment of smut in all media.

> The media cannot serve the public because they are organized to serve the advertiser. The media's real product is people. They deliver people to their clients, the advertisers.

An important distinguishing characteristic between the Traditional Journalist and the factor VI type individual—the Staunch Defender—is his lack of a feeling of intimidation by those critical of the press. Such a feeling, as will be seen later, borders on a feeling of paranoia on the Staunch Defender factor. A comparison of how each type views one particular statement might be helpful in illustrating this difference. The Traditional Journalist was the only type that agreed strongly with this statement: "I don't think that the media have been hampered in their presentation of news by the government criticism." The same statement got the strongest negative reaction by the Staunch Defender.

Even though the Traditional Journalist is quick to defend the press, there are some areas in which he concedes the need for government regulation. He believes that there should be a limit to the number of newspapers or broadcast stations a person can own and tends to agree that "limited regulation of the media gives important minority views the right to be heard."

Emphasis on this factor is placed on standing up for the press as it is today. The Traditional Journalist doesn't see the media as being corrupted by its establishmentarianism or as being culturally biased in favor of the middle and upper classes. Yet, he is willing to admit that all "corporations, including media, must assume more responsibility for what they do." He feels there is much room for improvement, but he is content with the media's general performance and is satisfied that the U.S. press system is functioning adequately.

Factor VI: The Staunch Defender

This factor was also dominated by persons with extensive media experience, but with a predominance of people with broadcasting backgrounds. Working broadcast journalists and newspaper publishers with broadcast experience were loaded highly on factor VI. This fact seems particularly relevant in a discussion of their attitudes toward the media because it is this group that showed the most defensiveness about their life's work and the role of the media in society. Statements that seemed to threaten the independence of the media or to infringe on their concept of First Amendment rights were ranked more negatively than any other factor.

The two major areas of concern for the Staunch Defender are government interference with the media and pressures from special interest groups to gain access to the press.

The first two statements ranked most highly by this group read as if they had been edited into a paragraph:

No government agency should be set up to determine what is authentic or biased in news reporting.

Once the government gets its foot in the door, even a little bit, government regulation of the media will grow. Eventually, we will have a press that is controlled by the government.

It is interesting to note that the latter statement was rated highly negative by the Critical Intellectual, neutral by the Revolutionary and the Traditional Journalist, positive by the Silent Majority, and extremely positive by the Staunch Defender.

The probroadcast nature of this factor is also signified by the high value this group placed on this statement:

If First Amendment principles are held not to apply to the broadcast media, it may well be that the constitution's guarantee of a free press is on its deathbed.

—and by their extreme negative reaction to this one:

The history of broadcasting in the U.S. is littered with the bodies of those who wanted to do something significant and who were driven out by the pimps and thieves who now run the media.

Curiously, the Traditional Journalist highly disagreed with the former statement while the Pro-Media Critic and the Revolutionary tended to agree, and the Silent Majority remained neutral.

Other highly ranked statements tend to shed some light on how the Staunch Defender visualizes his role in the media. He defends the commercial nature of the media by saying that "If it were not for the advertising dollar TV programing would be pathetic," and he admits that the media have a responsibility to "emphasize the good points of government policy." The only support for this view again came from the Silent Majority. Finally, a statement to which only the Critical Intellectual assigned a high positive value, but one which gains particular significance when agreed to by those in broadcasting, illustrates what the Revolutionary would call a rationalization for the commercial nature of the media:

> Broadcasting, as a mass commercial medium, has to give the majority of the people what they want, and what they want is entertainment and clever commercials.

Several statements illustrate the degree to which broadcasters feel intimidated by criticism and by those seeking access. This type rated the two following statements more positively than any other type:

> Although there is nothing basically wrong with pressure groups conveying their ideas and recommendations to media, their tactics are often reprehensible.

> The broadcasting system in the U.S. would be substantially destroyed or eroded if broadcasters are not provided with government protection against citizen pressure groups.

Statements with which this type disagreed more than any other type also indicate a feeling of intimidation:

> The press today seems paranoid. They call it free speech when they attack the government, but when government snaps back it's called intimidation.

> I don't think the media have been hampered in their presentation of news by the government criticism.

The extreme reaction to many of these comments seems to show a strong feeling of resentment toward those who would encroach on the rights of the media to make autonomous judgments about what is to be presented. The Staunch Defender is less ready to criticize the media than are the other types, and is more concerned with justifying the relationship between private enterprise and the mass media.

Even so, he is unwilling to assert that "The mass media should be completely free," and they believe that there should be definite "limitations on the number of newspapers or television stations that a person can own."

Implications

It is evident from this brief analysis that there is, to say the least, a wide divergence of opinion among the population as to exactly what the role of the media should be in today's society. Even within the ranks of the journalists there are differing views and priorities assigned to press problems. However, a few broad generalities did emerge from the study.

There is a general consensus on only a very few opinion statements, but even these provide some insight as to the general climate of opinion. The one item that all types agreed strongly with was one that seems to indicate the strength of the consumer movement: "Corporations, including media, must assume more responsibility for what they do."

Obviously, this statement could mean almost anything, depending on the individual. What is meant by "responsibility," and who is to judge when the proper level of responsibility has been achieved? These questions, of course, cannot be answered here, but the mere fact that such a vague statement was consistently rated high signifies that the problem of corporate irresponsibility is a pressing priority for a large segment of the American public. What is more significant is that the inclusion of the media in the statement did not deter the subjects from strongly agreeing. It would seem that most people nowadays see the media as another big business, subject to the failings of large corporate structures.

Adding to this implication is the fact that most of the respondents are not opposed to government regulation of the media to varying degrees. Only the Pro-Media Critic strongly agreed that "The mass media should be completely free," and even they contradicted this view by agreeing with other statements that imply government regulation is necessary. On the other hand, it is also significant that all types agreed strongly that "No government agency should be set up to determine what is authentic or biased in news reporting." This finding should comfort those in the media who fear too much government control, but should be compared to the general reaction to another statement:

> Once the government gets its foot in the door even a little bit, government regulation of the media will grow. Eventually, we will have a press that is controlled by the government.

Generally, people do not believe this statement; only the Silent Majority and the Staunch Defender rated it positively. The implication is obvious. The public is becoming more and more open to government regulation of the media in situations where such regulation is seen as beneficial to the public good. One such area, it seems, is the issue of minority access to the media. No type agreed with the statement that "Forcing minority opinions into a newspaper would be very harmful to the social good. It would epitomize social irresponsibility." Even the Staunch Defender rated this statement neutral, which is rather surprising. Historically, most Americans have been reluctant to allow any interference with the news judgment of the editor; this view has been held as one of the sacred implications of the First Amendment. Yet today, it seems, this view is definitely changing. The tendency is toward a new definition of that sacred gospel: "Freedom of the press, as expressed in the First Amendment, means freedom for every citizen to have access to the nation's media."

This statement was disagreed with by only two factions (the Silent Majority and the Pro-Media Critic) while the Staunch Defender and the Traditional Journalist rated it neutral and the Revolutionary and the Critical Intellectual strongly agreed. Speculation can only be made as to what the results would have been had this study been conducted ten years ago, but it is likely that the results would have been quite different.

Finally, it would not be stretching the point too far to say that the seeds for modification of our traditional concept of press freedom have been planted. Not only have they been planted, but the seedlings are popping out everywhere in the form of active criticism. Whether or not they will survive, and what the final consequences will be, is still unknown; nevertheless the signs are there from the inspection of those who must cope with the dilemma and make the decisions that will guide the future of our communications system.

Appendix E

TWO SURVEYS ON THE IMAGE OF THE NEWSPAPER

The first survey in this appendix is one conducted by J. Edward Murray in 1966, when he was managing editor of the *Arizona Republic.* It is reprinted here with Mr. Murray's permission. The survey was presented to the Associated Press Managing Editors Convention in San Diego, California, in 1966. It is unusual because Murray polled a dozen well-known newsmen and press critics for their views to an extended series of questions about the image of the newspaper. The second survey was conducted in 1969 by the APME Content Committee and is reprinted with permission of APME. The chairman was Robert P. Clark, of the Louisville *Times,* but the survey actually is composed of two surveys: one of how youth views the press, under Rene Cazanave, of the San Francisco *Examiner;* the other of how public officials and leaders viewed press performance compared with editors, conducted by Courtney R. Sheldon of the *Christian Science Monitor.*

ANSWERS TO A QUESTIONNAIRE ON IMAGE OF THE NEWSPAPER

In preparing a speech on the newspaper image and newspaper critics, I sent a questionnaire to a dozen men in the profession or on the edge of it.

These men didn't ask to be asked, and they didn't know their answers would be collected for distribution. I'm taking the liberty of distributing them because I think they represent excellent criticism.

I asked for even the briefest answers from those who were pressed for time, so please judge accordingly.

I include my own answers to each question first, because I sent them along with the original questionnaire to show the men who were getting it my own thinking, so they could agree or disagree in their answers. That is why some of the respondents refer to my position, or my answers, in some of theirs.

Here are the men who answered the questionnaire:

Harry Ashmore, chairman, Executive Committee, Board of Directors, Center for the Study of Democratic Institutions, Santa Barbara, California

Ben Bagdikian, critic, Columbia University

Dr. Chilton R. Bush, ANPA Research Consultant (retired executive head of department of journalism, Stanford University)

John H. Colburn, editor and publisher, Wichita *Eagle and Beacon*

Monty Curtis, executive director, American Press Institute

John S. Knight, publisher, Knight Newspapers

Carl Larsen, public relations director, University of Chicago

Rep. John E. Moss, chairman, Subcommittee on Foreign
Operations and Government Information
   Vermont Royster, editor, *Wall Street Journal*
   Stan Smith, general manager, American Newspaper
Publishers Association
   Russ Wiggins, editor, Washington *Post*

*Question 1: Have newspapers gained or lost in general
reputation, in prestige, in the confidence of their readers, in
the last two or three decades?*

Murray: I think newspapers have greatly improved since
World War II, and so I think they are more highly regarded by
discerning readers. And there are more such because the
level of education is rising.
   With the less discerning reader, possibly the average
one, I think the carping about newspapers is at roughly the
same level it has always been.

Ashmore: If general reputation and prestige can be translated
into influence, they have unquestionably fallen into second
place to TV and radio. In this regard the question does not
turn on the confidence of their readers, but the amount of
attention they are able to attract.
   I suspect the serious readers who are left may have a
little more confidence in the fewer and more sedate
newspapers than they had in their more flamboyant and
competitive predecessors.

Bush: Gained. Three decades ago Harold Ickes and
F. D. Roosevelt were criticizing the one-party press, and so
did Adlai Stevenson as late as 1952. Herbert Brucker wrote in
1951: "The citizen regards (the newspaper) as a big,
powerful, and remote entity, with motives and interests that
may well be different from his own. He has just as much
interest in freedom *from* the press as he has in freedom *of*
the press" (*Freedom of Information,* p. 70).
   Certain leading "authoritarian" publishers have died and
their successors have published fair newspapers.

The quadrennial poll of *Editor & Publisher* has shown a steadily declining proportion of newspapers supporting the Republican candidate for President. My test [*Note:* a standardized formula for measuring public attitude toward a newspaper] was used by two newspapers in 1964 which had always supported the Republican candidate, but which supported Johnson in 1964. Almost the only readers in the sample who disapproved of these newspapers were the ultra-right-wing Republican readers. I believe the public now recognizes that most newspapers are fair.

I asked Herb [Herbert Brucker] if he still thought his statement was correct. He said that the better educated people still perceive the newspaper as an entity that is not responsible to anybody.

Colburn: More newspapers have the confidence of the people today than they did thirty years ago. As more people get better acquainted with newspapers, they better appreciate the problem of handling complicated information on a schedule of constant deadline pressures. Many of them marvel that we do as well as we do. In some cases, too many people are overconfident in their analysis of newspapers. They fail to read critically the qualifications that appear in many stories. They are inclined to accept a qualified situation as an unqualified fact and this attitude places a tremendous responsibility on the newspaper to make attribution as precise and clear as possible. We need to encourage people to read more critically for their own better understanding.

Curtis: Generalizations mislead. Reserve that trap for peripheral critics.

Good newspapers have gained in reputation, prestige, and reader confidence. They always have. Evidence: increasing response by readers to advertising in newspapers which earn their trust; increase in reader participation through response to public-service campaigns, letters to the editor, forum discussions, such favorable comments of readers on these, etc.

Bad and mediocre newspapers have lost any reputation

or reader confidence they had. Many are dead in larger cities. Those surviving do so because they are the only print outlet for local retail advertising. They are read for little else. (The latter group receives more attention because sin is more interesting than virtue, especially to peripheral critics who are so much more articulate than the 61 million people who buy newspapers daily, but so much less important.)

Larsen: It is difficult to generalize about the reputations of newspapers. In the intellectual community there appears to be contentment with the products of the New York *Times*, the Washington *Post*, and the Los Angeles *Times*, the Milwaukee *Journal*, the Louisville *Courier-Journal*, and other major urban newspapers. On the other hand, there is concern that some newspapers serving isolated and monopoly situations are not doing as well as they might in providing significant, hard news with qualified opinion to their readers. In totality, however, it is my impression that newspapers have improved since World War II—perhaps because publishers and editors have become smarter and their readers have higher educational levels. As for the confidence of their readers, it is my impression, too, that some newspapers have risen in this respect while others have declined.

Moss: I feel they have lost reputation for objectivity with their readers.

Royster: If there is a gain or loss it would be impossible to measure. My guess is there has been very little change since John Peter Zenger.

Smith: Going back three decades reaches a point *before* World War II. The newspapers did such a wonderful job of covering World War II without endangering national security that I think the answer would be a very great gain if we compare 1966 with 1936.

If we consider only two decades and the postwar period only, I still think the performance of newspapers has been showing such steady improvement that even irresponsible criticism has caused no loss of general reputation with readers. It is important to note that the general level of reader education has greatly increased and, therefore, newspapers must improve as their readers' tastes improve.

Wiggins: Gained.

Bagdikian: The role of the newspaper in the life of the individual reader and in society as a whole has changed so much it is hard to generalize about its general reputation today and thirty years ago. But when you put it in contemporary terms, you have to ask "better than what?" Better than radio-TV? Not so fast, dramatic or literal. Better than news magazines? Not so readable or quick. Better than books? Not so comprehensive. Better than that college course in economics and social history? Not so sophisticated or sound. Better than the last PTA meeting or city council meeting? Not so engaging. Yet all these things have, in the last twenty years, become common influences among newspaper readers. So readers have far more exacting demands on their newspapers, higher standards of judgment and more urgent needs. This is why newspapers are better than they used to be but they have lost ground in the eyes of readers, sometimes in quality and sometimes in simple relevance.

Knight: I dislike lumping things together, and particularly so in the field of communications.

There are excellent and poor radio stations, exciting and dull magazines, provocative public speakers and also the "egg-layers." So it is with newspapers. The good ones are responsible purveyors of information, protect the public interest through investigative reporting, and express their own opinions with clarity and conviction.

The best newspapers, and these are not limited to lists prepared by the traditionalists, have gained in general reputation, prestige, and confidence of readers in the last two or three decades.

Newspapers of the counting-house variety—dull, inert, and unconcerned—have neither gained nor lost. In metropolitan cities, they suffer from malnutrition, and are gradually engulfed in the merger tide. Those without competition generally prosper because the reader has no other choice, and is resigned to his fate.

Question 2: If there has been a marked change, what are some of the main reasons?

Murray: The marked change has been the improvement in the newspapers, and it has been caused mainly by competition from radio and TV and from the news magazines.

The technological revolution is pushing newspapers into great improvements in the transmission and presentation of news.

Ashmore: Implied in question 1.

Bush: See answer to question 1.

Colburn: Perhaps the biggest reason is that fewer newspapers take what was once interpreted as the sensational approach. No longer do we have "extras" based on fragmentary and often irresponsible first reports. More important, newspapers today deal in wider areas of information that the reader can associate himself with personally—stock-market information, modern living—from patio construction to menus—trends in education, science, medicine, and many others. Also, newspapers are less blatantly partisan, more universal than parochial in their outlook, and the growing number of good ones that offer a variety of outlook creates an attitude of respect even though the reader may dislike many of the paper's policies.

Curtis: Good newspapers gain because editors stay close to readers and employes; modernize content and packaging; expand news fields; write for today's intelligent audience;

produce vigorous editorial pages; spend money wisely on coverage; suppress nothing; and meet today's challenge of excellence.

Bad newspapers lose because of a shoddy, smeary product; news suppression and slanting; excessive reliance upon syndicated junk because it is cheap; underestimating today's audience; low salaries; disrespect for news and excessive love of features; repulsively bad taste; but why go on? They are dead or dying.

Larsen:

(a) Better-educated editors and reporters.

(b) The fact that publishing good newspapers is good business just as good government is good politics.

(c) Competition from electronic journalism—radio (AM-FM) and television (VHF-UHF, Educational). And, finally, improved periodicals including the news magazines. On a sociological note, it might be noted that national periodicals such as *Time, Newsweek,* and the *National Observer* have become subtle pressures on local editors to improve their newspapers because they not only are competing for subscriptions but also for the reader's time. Yes, the technological revolution is pushing newspapers into great improvements in the transmission and presentation of news. But nothing beats good writing, honest reporting, and intelligent editing.

Moss: Less competition, in other words too many one-newspaper communities.

Larger less personal organizations, too few owned by active personally involved ownership.

Too strong an urge to conform—to avoid offense—in other words the day of the great editors seems over.

Royster: See question 1.

Smith: Readers are more perceptive today than ever before, as indicated in my answer to question 1.

Wiggins: Better coverage—more advertising.

Bagdikian: Newspapers continue to be owned and too often run by men who are not close enough to those great big confusing changes in the outside world. There are too many papers that continue to sell mainly because of their ads, TV listings, and the top two wire stories, but whose owners think they sell because the paper is a first-rate newspaper. When outside papers of better quality, news magazines, books, weekly and monthly reviews, and TV begin draining away the attention of his most profitable readers, the typical owner reverts to such idiocy as those cartoons telling the reader how good newspapers are. Remember "Movies Are Better Than Ever?" Which didn't work. And then movies did get better than ever and the slogans weren't needed anymore?

Knight: Here again, modern, resourceful and enlightened newspaper managements have brought marked improvements to their publications. Vastly improved writing, attractive typography, and exciting published techniques are readily apparent to the reader.

Editorial policies which reason rather than instruct, which present fairly all sides of an issue, which respect the reader's point of view, do indeed win his confidence.

Newspapers which are didactic, strident in tone, and indurated to criticism can win no new friends, but only harden the beliefs of those who already agree.

Question 3: Is there more or less criticism of newspapers now than in the past?

Murray: I don't know. Possibly more.

Ashmore: I see no significant change—but I suspect it is less, which may mean no more than that people are less concerned with the impact and influence of newspapers now that they no longer control the mass media market.

Bush: On the whole, there is less criticism. Very little of it now is criticism of "authoritarianism," but it is more sophisticated. It is criticism of the shortcomings of the newspaper in nonpolitical areas. Last night, for example, the educational TV program was critical of the vulgarity of the newspaper: too much sex. The newspaper is also criticized for giving less space to the cultural sphere of life.

Curtis: Less criticism of good newspapers by readers. How long has it been since you heard: "You can't believe what you read in the newspapers." Or: "It is just newspaper talk." In the 20s I heard those phrases daily. They have almost disappeared in cities with good newspapers. You still hear them in communities with bad newspapers. (The editors of these newspapers avoid APME, ASNE, and API. Let us rejoice.)

More criticism of all newspapers from the peripheral professional critics. One cause is the efforts of television, radio and some national magazines to downgrade newspapers in the battle for circulation and national advertising. Be realistic. You cannot expect national TV, radio, and magazines to say anything very good about newspapers, or at least very loud or very often. We are competitors. I know of a recent case when a responsible article by an informed and excellent writer was rejected by a magazine because the balanced picture was favorable to newspapers. An honest story on newspapers was in *Business Week* recently. Occasionally there is an honest article in national magazines about a single newspaper but when the critics paint with a broad brush, like the juvenile and almost factless distortions in *Newsweek* last fall, the magazines usually make newspapers generally look as bad as possible. It is their racket. It is up to us to take care of ours.

Colburn: Percentagewise, probably not much change. Hard to measure. However, probably the criticism gets more attention today than it did years ago. In some cases, newspapers may well be oversensitive to criticism from an articulate minority that may be more interested in its own biases than in the public interest. In certain other cases, some newspapers may react defensively ("Don't tell me how to run my business"), or react negatively instead of positively. Overall, I doubt if the press is any more criticized than the churches, as a group, the education establishments, TV-radio, the medical profession, or the bar and judiciary. This despite the fact that our mistakes are displayed more prominently.

Larsen: I would suppose that there is more criticism of newspapers as the critics become more articulate and better educated. I am unaware of any significant organized criticism, however.

Moss: More as TV and radio report events—especially political events—in greater detail and with less partisan flavor.

Royster: My guess is "about the same." Remember the blasts about "yellow journalism."

Smith: Less criticism than in the early days of the Republic when it was particularly violent. More criticism than at some stages in our history. Probably about the same now as in most periods of our history.

Wiggins: Less.

Bagdikian: I don't know. My guess is that there is more technical and particularized criticism—the sessions on makeup, communication, etc.—and less general social criticism. Also, what criticism there is of a general kind tends to get a different kind of exposure than before, through competing mass media.

Knight: No more ill-tempered criticism, perhaps, than in the past. And certainly not as much as in the days of personal journalism. Yet we hear and receive more complaints if only because communications are vastly improved.
  Newspapers are widely discussed in magazines,

pamphlets, on radio and television. They have a deep fascination for the critics, and, in a way, this is a tribute to newspaper vitality.

Much of the criticism is pure piffle, yet some of the barbs directed against newspapers find their mark, and this is good for our souls.

Question 4: Who are some of the main newspaper critics?

Murray:
—Newspaper editors who are running scared and rightly so.

—The American Press Institute, the Nieman Fellows, the *Columbia Review,* and a growing number of other postgraduate professional groups concerned with news presentation.

—Ben Bagdikian and Harry Ashmore.

—Lawyers because of the Free Press/Fair Trial controversy.

—University professors, who often want newspapers to serve only their best-educated readers.

—Scientists, doctors, and other professionals who mistakenly want the newspapers to meet their own particular level of expertise.

—The Berkeley-age protest generation who think the popular press generally is the willing slave of the status quo.

—Politicians who use the press as a whipping boy because it opposes them or their newest nostrums.

—The unthinking reader who objects to unpleasant news on the theory that it will go away if unnoticed.

—Sports fans, club women, society groups, other special groups, who can no longer get their own special news in the paper because of space limitations.

—The average intelligent citizen, who is better educated and has a much greater spectrum of interest than ever before, but somehow finds that his newspaper doesn't satisfy him: the things he's interested in are not reported well enough, even though there are many more things reported than he has time to be interested in.

Ashmore: Your list is fairly complete. It may be worthy of note that you can mention only two, Bagdikian and me, by name, and for me, at least, the critical function is a peripheral activity performed as a kind of perverse labor of love. I don't think there are any effective critics of the communications media, which is why I keep plugging away for some version of the old Commission on a Free and Responsible Press.

I am convinced from experience and from study of the record that newspapers and broadcasting are incapable of self-criticism or self-regulation.

So far the journalism schools have proved incapable of anything more than heavy-handed and fuzzy research, and I think they are too closely tied to the business to perform a genuine critical function. The academic community in general provides some effective, if esoteric criticism at the moral and esthetic level, but is generally too far removed from the sweaty reality with which the mass media must deal.

Bush: In addition to those you mentioned, there is still considerable criticism of newspapers in the labor-union journals.

Colburn: You mean locally, nationally? Generally, certain intellectuals seeking or having easy answers to problems that do not lend themselves to quick solutions; thin-skinned politicians who make a fetish of attacking the press to gain attention; many people whose own selfish interests are adversely affected by information newspapers bring to public attention.

Curtis: Ben Bagdikian is the equal of the late Joe Liebling as the most interesting, the best writer, and the least helpful. It is tough to make a living as a free-lance press critic.

John Tebbel in the *Saturday Review of Literature* is consistently dull and uninformed.

Curtis: The little fellows spawned and fed at the Hutchins hatchery in Santa Barbara fling a barb now and then. They are unimportant and insofar as I can learn from newspaper readers, unknown.

Whatever happened to Jack Paar?

Far too many professors in low-grade journalism schools who were fired from newspaper staffs as incompetent turned to teaching and are resentful. They are unimportant to general readers, but an evil influence on students. All of us know young newspaper people come out of these schools despising newspapers. This is a disappearing group of newspaper critics as journalism schools continue to raise salaries and recruit successes rather than failures. There was a time when salaries were so low that the schools could not hire successful newspapermen—and God knows newspaper salaries were low enough in those days. There are many excellent journalism professors who can make valid and helpful criticisms of newspapers. You know who they are when newspaper owners hire them in the summer to critique their newspapers.

There are two other groups of critics, by far the most important, and they are the answer to question 5.

Larsen: Intelligent newspaper editors and concerned reporters determined to improve their products and also to survive as the communications war develops.

Academicians—especially in the social sciences—who use the daily press for resource material.

The legal community which, for some strange reason, views the press as an enemy while protecting an inefficient, often corrupt court system that the press ignores.

Certainly, the American Press Institute and the Nieman Fellows at Harvard and the new academic program at Stanford for graduate journalists serve as critics of the press. Hopefully, much of their criticism will be constructive. A profession with the public obligation of the press should welcome, not deplore, such criticism and attempt to implement suggestions that are valid. I feel that you should not be overly concerned by pressure-group criticism, but rather should treat more seriously competent criticism offered by qualified professionals in journalism, mass communications and the academic community.

General-circulation newspapers cannot please everyone and they would be reduced to pablum if they tried. Some of the nation's most successful journals—*Time, Newsweek, Wall Street Journal*—all have their points of view and you either take it or leave it. And, here I define "successful" as having impact on the leadership community—not the followers—as well as being "successful" for the publishers in economic terms.

Moss: The average John Q, who feels in too many instances the paper is big business and has an axe to grind when it takes a position or states an opinion.

Royster: Newspaper editors; we are great people for self-flaggellation. A worthy trait.

Lawyers and politicians, both groups preferring that newspapers publish only what they themselves want published.

Smith: In order of their validity; that is, the most valid listed first: readers; editors and publishers; some, but not all journalism school deans; a few, but not many politicians.

Wiggins: Lawyers.

Bagdikian:

—The various exercises in editorial masochism (APME, NCEW, API, etc.), but all internal
—Organized constituents of the press—bar associations, lobbies, politicians
—Academics
—Ideologues
—Working press groups, like ANG
—Some departments of journalism

Knight: Politicians, public officials, bar associations, news magazines, retired editors, writers who specialize in this field, television commentators who "review the press," professional groups, the *Columbia Review,* angry clubwomen, and just readers—bless them—who take pen in hand to vent their displeasure.

The editor who isn't regularly taken to the woodshed should be running a trade publication.

Question 5: What are some of the most valid criticisms?

Murray:

—Important news, and especially complex news, is served raw, without being put into context. This is especially bad for young readers who lack background for much of the news.

—Complex news, which is increasing, is still reported by writers with too little specialized knowledge of their own.

—Despite the deluge of important and useful news close to home, we still use oceans of space and reader time on second-rate, far-off catastrophe, crime, and meaningless political crisis.

—Although newspapers are trying, and doing better, they are still failing in their responsibility to give readers the information they need to be good citizens, to cope with change.

—The reporters for most newspapers, and often for the wire services, are as yet unequal to the gargantuan task of analyzing and reporting Big Government, Big Science, Big Business, and Big Labor adequately enough so that the average citizen can understand and act intelligently in a representative democracy.

Ashmore: I would endorse your list and add one count: With only a few exceptions, the newspapers I see regularly seem to me to be rapidly or gradually defaulting on their obligations as independent advocates on public matters. I don't mean old-fashioned hell-raising for the sake of hell-raising (and circulation) but sober, consistent espousal of realistic courses of action that are, almost by definition, either neglected or unpopular, or both. (If the cause is popular it doesn't need an advocate.) What makes this so tough is that the newspapers are inevitably linked economically and otherwise to the interests that dominate their community. Yet if the newspapers do not speak out against these interests, when need be, who will? Not broadcasting, certainly. Except for the now unusual circumstance of the individually or family-owned newspaper that is willing out of pride, tradition, or simply eccentricity to play the maverick role, the whole of the press seems to be sinking into the painless, nonwave-making, on-the-other-hand style that seems to be the heritage of the corporate character that dominates broadcasting.

Bush: Most newspapers are defaulting in their responsibility for explaining how our economic system operates. Very few editorial writers are equipped to write in this field. They are too lazy intellectually to think through those government and business policies that cause inflation. They are chosen usually because they are "writers." So they write mainly about matters (other than local and regional) that are less important than economics.

Nor do some news editors know how to select and display economic news. If such news has a dollar sign, it goes in the financial section. (This week in my newspaper a story about the bank-deposit guarantee being raised to $15,000 and the reply of the chairman of the President's Business Council to the propaganda of housewives boycotting food retailers were displayed where only investors read them. The same paper did the same thing the last time the Treasury increased the interest rate on E and H bonds.)

The less that readers know about the operation of our business and government fiscal and monetary policies, the more there is an opportunity for demagogues to be elected and to legislate stupid economic measures.

Colburn: The most valid criticism is that dealing with

judgment. Knowledge doesn't always make for wisdom and too many of our goofs can be attributed to lack of judgment and wisdom. Deadline pressures too often prompt supervising editors to pass copy that should be held up for more research. Not enough time is taken to probe all aspects of a story before going into print with it; too often the "other side" is dealt with only superficially because the writer runs into difficulty getting information. Many writers try for the "headline" angle rather than attempting to determine what really is the important substance.

Curtis: For twenty years API has worked with two groups of helpful, vigorous critics. (We also tried the professional critics but they were unrealistic, unhelpful and given to generalizations.) Our two groups have that rare charm of knowing what they are talking about. These groups are:

1. Intelligent readers not connected with any form of journalism. Good newspapermen report their criticisms at API Seminars.

2. Thinking, experienced, devoted newspapermen who *read* many newspapers.

What are their *valid* criticisms?

—Newspapers in many large cities are too big. There is an increase in circulation stops with this complaint. Many readers, especially young couples, do not have time for a 100-page newspaper. Regardless of good packaging, attractive makeup, and many sections to choose from, the bulk is forbidding. We know what these people will turn to——, and at less cost in money and time, but at a severe loss in developing as informed, thoughtful citizens.

—Many individual news stories are too long. Too much background is repeated. These critics ask: When there is a situation developing day by day in tiny, dull steps, why print them? Wait until there is something worth reading.

—Some individual news stories (especially local) are too short. They lack detail. Smart-aleck feature writing is no substitute for basic reporting. (Some dead papers, especially in New York, specialized in this field.)

—Failure on the part of some papers (by no means all) to plumb deeply into vital local situations. Many readers in some cities were shocked when race riots exploded and newspapers had not been reporting conditions which caused the riots. Those newspapers had been asleep to a local news situation. Such reporting would not necessarily have prevented riots, but the newspaper image would not have suffered. There is too much stable-door-locking in such situations.

Larsen: You frequently must read two accounts of the same event from, say, a newspaper and a magazine, to obtain a meaningful understanding of the event. This is because the selection of major news is so subjective and depends, more often than not, on the academic competence of the editor, not of the reader. And, the competence of the editor relates finally to how much the publisher is willing to pay for a good editor.

The lack of specialization for reporters: a hangover from the depression-age theory that only good generalists are needed in city rooms. How many James Restons or Eddie Laheys does a society such as ours develop for journalism? And could they cover a complex story concerned, say, with microbiological research?

The view that newspapers, while often doing impressive jobs overseas or in Washington with their reportage, neglect the controversial home-front stories for Chamber of Commerce reasons. Example: In Chicago, for years, the newspaper played down racial disturbances under the theory that extensive coverage would only contribute to their seriousness and in the naive hope that things would get better in the absence of any planned reform. Then came radio-TV, which aggressively covered such events (especially last summer) and forced the newspapers to put on page one the stories they formerly buried on page 26. In the 1950s, one had to read the *New York Times* for accounts of what was happening in Chicago. It was ironic to hear of editors arguing

for freedom of information while they were denying it to
their readers—their customers. Is there any wonder that
some circulations have fallen as the readers found news—not
as significant, but less tampered with—on the major TV
stations?

Moss:

—Fear of controversy.
—The inability to become indignant over infringement
on rights of constitutional character.
—Too little real competition in the political and social
areas. How many prolabor or even neutral papers are there?

Royster:

—A tendency to center news stories on the most
provocative of events (or the speaker's remarks, etc.)
—Serving up "raw news"—or simply the "facts"—when
often the raw news can be misleading
—Timidity with the "complicated" story
—An overabundance of trivia

Smith: Our inability sometimes to put related events into the
proper perspective within the time limitations of daily
publication. This can never be achieved to perfection but it is
one of our real problems and technology cannot solve it.
Only hard work by reporters and editors can do this job.
Related to the above and adopting your own comment, I
agree that we have not yet found out how to convey to the
average citizen a real understanding of the function of Big
Government, Big Labor, Big Business, and Big Science. We
need to do this desperately because these are real problems
for the country and they are not very well understood.

Wiggins:

—Poor coverage of courts
—Inadequate national news coverage

—Insufficient local stuff and expertise
—Weak editorial pages
—Neglect of "other side of tracks"
—Technological lag in production methods

Bagdikian:

1. Newspapers are poorly edited, by which I mean that there are not enough editors in authority who have enough knowledge, high enough standards and dedication to turn out a daily product that meets contemporary expectations.

2. Not enough talent is retained and developed by newspapers. The first reason is because most papers do such a poor job that a bright young man or woman can't conceive of spending his life at it. The second is that most papers continue to pay reporters as though they were superannuated copyboys, circa 1950.

3. Most papers have been backward in grappling with their technological problems, which, unsolved, limit the energy and attention the paper's leadership put into the substance of their product.

Knight: Superficial handling of significant news, absence of adequate and informative (including maps) background material, sloppy headline writing, inept handling of pictures, lack of humor, bland editorials, weak local coverage, too little emphasis upon investigative reporting, and too much reliance on syndicated columnists.

As one critic said recently, the new newspaper in New York reminds me of "an acre of creampuffs."

Today's newspapers suffer also from conformity. For instance, only a handful have opposed our involvement in Vietnam. As with the U.S. Senate, most accept the government line. On this issue, as with others, we need more dissent, not less.

These are not "outside" criticisms, but my own.

Question 6: Are there other groups in the society, who, for selfish reasons, unfairly criticize the newspapers? The government? Television and radio? Magazines? University professors? Others?

Murray: I suppose there is some substantial criticism, as indicated under question 4. I think if we would report it more intelligently, we would expose it for what it is, and maybe even tell our own story a little better in the process.

Ashmore: This is true of all those cited above, and others, but individually and collectively I have never thought it mattered much. I doubt, on balance, if the newspapers receive as much unfair criticism as they dish out, and as an editor I never considered that I had the right to demand quarter.

Bush: The government? The newspaper is a natural enemy of the politician.

University professors? Most of them lack a critical faculty and embrace the idea.

Others? Teachers of journalism exposed to a local newspaper that is inadequate; their criticism is often justified.

Colburn: These groups are no different than others. Much of the criticism of newspapers misses the mark because it is motivated by selfish, competitive, or political reasons. Too often we are too timid to throw the publicity spotlight on charlatans; and because of poor judgment give unwarranted or, at times, even offensive publicity to people.

Curtis: The government? Yes, national, state, and local. It is eternal. I hope it never stops. Who, or what, other than a good newspaper, stands between the government and the people; between the courts and the people; between the police and the people; between ownership and management and the people; between labor leaders and the people; between the church and the people; in fact, between all the wielders of power and those upon whom they would wield it for selfish ends?

Television and radio? Yes, it will become worse as

television settles into a routine like radio and the battle for public attention and advertising income becomes more desperate.

Magazines? Yes. It is a mixed bag. A few are fair, a considerable number unfair, and most poorly informed.

University professors? I hear little criticism from professors who have the good fortune to live in cities where there are excellent newspapers. I hear considerable criticisms from professors in cities or towns where there are bad newspapers.

Others? Yes. Some ministers. Many unendorsed candidates. Bleeders for causes. Bless 'em all. They are readers. There is a category of unfair criticism to our advantage. When there is a hot local issue (zoning, location of a new highway, etc.) people take sides and raise hell. Good newspapers publish all sides of the argument, keep news columns scrupulously clean, and take their own vigorous position in editorials. Impartial news coverage offends many aroused readers but we have a good competitive tool here. Try telling these people to take their arguments to television and radio. They will tell you that television and radio are not as good for them as print. Viewers may be stirred for a few minutes but this fades. Print remains.

Larsen: This is a difficult question to answer without deep and significant research. What is "unfair" and what is "criticism"? A free press must expect to be criticized frequently as it makes highly subjective choices about news values and investigative stories. Certainly, political leaders and other vested interests will use criticism—both fair and unfair—as a weapon against a free but responsible press which seeks to alert the public to their excuses.

Moss: All do when it suits their purposes.

Royster: No answer.

Smith: I do not think there are very many "groups" who

deliberately do this. I am unwilling to generalize in such criticism of "the government, television and radio, magazines, university professors, or others." There are some individuals in all the above categories who unfairly criticize newspapers (and criticize other media also) for their own selfish reasons but I think they are a minority. I think some people in the press pay too much attention to unfair criticism and overreact. This has a reverse effect, in my opinion.

Wiggins: Magazines.

Bagdikian: Various parts of all these categories criticize the press for selfish reasons, sometimes fairly and sometimes unfairly.

Knight: Yes. Government at all levels often engages in unfair criticism, and usually when a newspaper is uncovering a development officialdom would like to conceal.

I have no complaint about radio and television, except in the instances where a radio "newsman" lifts his information from our printed editions. Television news programs have shown much improvement. The stations which editorialize are eager, if not skilled practicioners of that art.

Time and *Newsweek* delight in belittling the newspapers in what I described as a "mischievous melange of misusage and misinformation." It is one of the oldies in their field and can be endured.

No trouble from professors. But spare us from the apoplectic alumni who go into a rage whenever their university permits freedom of expression on unpopular subjects, or fails to discipline students demonstrating against the war in Vietnam.

Question 7: Is the credibility of newspapers being dangerously eroded by the critics?

Murray: I don't know. I don't think so, however.

Ashmore: No.

Bush: No. But the newspapers can do a better job in the public schools of explaining the objectives and limitations of newspapers.

Colburn: Another area difficult to measure, but I doubt it. People have a habit of reading into copy what they want to read—or hearing what they want to hear from a speaker.

Curtis: Not by the professionals. Their approach to the subject is dull to the general reader. The newspaper which renders a necessary, honest, and interesting service to the reader every day has nothing to worry about from the pros. In the heyday of Joe Liebling I once asked thirty-two newspaper readers of high educational, economic, and social level: "What do you think about Joe Liebling?" All of them said, "Who is Joe?" Now they say, "Who is Ben?"

I don't know what effect these people really have. Back in 1960 when Carl Lindstrom wrote his churlish *The Fading American Newspaper* the national daily circulation of ABC newspapers was 58,299,723. Five years later, despite increased prices, disappearance of bad metropolitan dailies, mergers, long strikes in big cities, and high mobility of population, we had faded upward to 60,350,000. Much more important is the constant increase in the quality and number of good newspapers. Did Carl have anything to do with it? I don't know.

Recently there was a television show, "The Vanishing Newspaper." I watched it. Careful inquiry among nonnewspaper friends disclosed no one who watched it. In the winter of 1947–48 we had a radio program, "CBS Views the Press." It died for lack of listener interest. Professional-press criticism bores the general public. Local-reader criticism fascinates the general public. When a newspaperman meets his community friends there is one subject they will always raise—the local newspaper.

Larsen: The credibility of newspapers is in the hands of the publishers, editors, reporters, editorial writers, etc., just as the integrity of Corn Flakes is in the hands of the makers.

Newspapers in a free society must accept criticism with sophistication and use truth as their weapon in rebutting such attacks.

Moss: Not yet—but the limit is in prospect.

Royster: No.

Smith: I do not think so.

Wiggins: No.

Bagdikian: John Williams (Rep.-Del.) has an observation that I think of as Williams' Law; "It isn't the criticism that hurts so much; it's the response to the criticism." Senator Williams has sent a few people to jail to prove the soundness of his aphorism.

I don't think credibility of newspapers is being dangerously eroded by the critics. It is being *dangerously* eroded by the vulnerability of newspapers combined with their insensitivity.

Knight: No, I don't think so, although the self-serving radio and television surveys would so indicate. But here again, we have a generalization. What newspapers?

Question 8: Are newspapers too little or too much concerned with their character and reputation? With their image? With their critics?

Murray: Newspapers can't be too concerned with their character and reputation; the competition is rough.

I think we might do a better job in presenting our story, and so help our image. We seem to err either on the side of being patently too self-serving about the obvious or shyly self-conscious about actual virtue.

Ashmore: They damned well ought to be concerned about their character. Their reputation, too, subject to Jonathan

Daniels' notable stricture that journalism is *not* a respectable business—meaning respectable as it might be defined by the admissions committee of the country club. If a newspaper has genuine integrity coupled with high professional skill and adequate resources, it will make its own image—and will have no real need for public relations specialists and promotion men. And it should delight in its critics, by whom it will be known.

Bush: The industry doesn't seem to know how to improve its image. A great opportunity has been missed by the mishandling of National Newspaper Week. The task of preparing office ads is turned over to an ad agency which knows almost nothing about the function and role of the newspaper. Suppose that a teacher of journalism who has specialized in the history and the law of the press had prepared the ads, devoting each one to the story of an editor, a publisher, who fought for the liberties of the press (e.g., John Wilkes) and to certain Supreme Court decisions that have upheld the rights and privileges of the press. And some of the crusades and campaigns of the press in behalf of the people. Such stories (in the form of ads) would probably be well read and understood.

That a good many newspapers are concerned with their image is shown by the considerable number of publishers who have administered the public-attitudes test that we developed.

Newspapers are also aware of the rise in the level of education of their readers.

Colburn: Some have been too little concerned with their own self-evaluation; too blasé about their responsibilities to their own community. During the past ten years, however, the encouraging trend has been toward improvement of the news and information products; more awareness of the difference between public curiosity and legitimate public interest; more awareness of the newspaper's responsibility to provide information that can aid public discussion and understanding of vital public issues.

Curtis: Good newspapers are deeply concerned, now as always. For many, many years fine newspapermen have contributed daily to building newspaper character and reputation. They still do. They always will as long as we nurture the breed.

Bad newspapers never did give a damn about their character and reputation. As long as they were making money, nothing else made much difference. The places where they can make money have almost disappeared. Most have died or lost identity in a merger. Better education and improved public taste led the readers to superior competitors.

With their image? Same as above. Every correctly spelled name, every piece of honest reporting, of good writing, of reasoned editorial position, of interesting content, of unsuppressed news, of unslanted news, of service to the community, of honest advertising, improves our image. Otherwise, otherwise.

With their critics? Good newspapers are deeply concerned with valid criticism. Good newspapermen profit by it.

Larsen: I agree with J. Edward Murray that newspapers cannot be too concerned with their character and reputations. Like individuals, they must preserve their integrity in the face of persons who would like to use them to further their own ends.

I would not worry too much about the image of newspapers, in a public relations sense. Images should only be true reflections of events and products as they really are, not as you would like them to be. Your colleagues should work on the product, not the image.

Moss: Too little or too much concerned with their character and reputation? No.

With their image? Yes.

With their critics? No.

Royster: Yes, in the sense of seeking public relations

gimmicks to improve their "image." No, in the sense of worrying about how to make newspapers better.

Smith: Nothing is more important than the *character* of a newspaper. When the publisher and editor do a first-rate job of building the character of a newspaper, there need be no worries about its reputation, image or its critics. As I indicated above, I think some newspaper *people* are sometimes too much concerned with unfair criticism. Of course, some people are too little concerned with valid criticism.

Wiggins: I don't know.

Bagdikian: It's the trollop who talks most about her virtue. Where can a paper be hurt by criticism? Ad agencies, but their computers don't read. And the newspaper's own readers (and if the paper keeps its readers' loyalties, the agencies will at least read the numbers). How can a first-rate newspaper that is seen every day by its readers be hurt by an outsider telling them that their first-rate newspaper is no good?

Knight: Perceptive editors are sensitively attuned to slurs against their character and reputation. These should be answered, not ignored. Many newspapers are not sufficiently concerned, either with their image, or with their critics.

Question 9: Has the growth in monopoly newspaper operation hurt or helped the image of newspapers?

Murray: I think monopoly, for the most part, has helped the quality of newspapers and hurt their image.

Ashmore: The *fact* of monopoly ownership is still regarded as potentially dangerous by many, and is resented by all those who, rightly or wrongly, feel that they are being abused or inadequately served by the newspapers. The *result* of monopoly in most cases has been a considerable improvement in the product as a result of greater resources and the abandonment of bad practices brought on by competition. I doubt that the change in image is significant, either way.

Bush: I agree with your answer to this question. Of course, the reason for monopoly newspapers is that their competitors were poorly managed and spent less money on their product, which is exactly why some brands of products have outsold competing brands.

Eventually, the public will adjust to the monopoly situation to the extent that all newspapers are serious, informative and tolerant; and that day may not be far away.

Colburn: Lack of competition in the newspaper field has made more responsible newspapers, in most areas. Many—probably too many—exceptions still can be found, and generally these exceptions provide little more than pablum to their readers.

Curtis: There has been little harm to honest, excellent newspapers. All of us who have worked in both competitive and monopoly situations know that you can do a better job when you don't lower your standards to meet low competition. It all depends upon the integrity, desires, ambitions and abilities of ownership. You can have excellent monopoly newspapers and you can have dreadful monopoly newspapers. The former are not hurt. The latter sink a little more each year.

Larsen: Again, I agree with JEM. In many monopoly cities—Minneapolis, Des Moines—the newspapers are much better than they are in cities with heavy competition.

Moss: Hurt.

Royster: In many cases has improved newspaper operations. I doubt it has affected the "image" much one way or the other.

Smith: I dislike the word "monopoly" because no newspaper has an actual monopoly, as there are many other sources of news in any community and certainly many competitors for advertising. If the single-ownership situation results in the production of a better newspaper, I think readers are very little concerned with the alleged "monopoly." This is demonstrated in many cities.

Wiggins: Monopoly newspaper operation may have one effect in one city and another effect in another and hardly no public reaction at all in the communities that do not have monopoly newspapers.

Bagdikian: It has hurt but it is a diminishing hurt. Most people have never known truly competitive dailies and are coming to accept their local daily as they do their local telephone company, as though ordained to be a monopoly.

Knight: Newspapers without other newspaper competition either strive for improvement or grow as dull as their owners. It all depends on whether the owner takes pride in his publication and is aware of his responsibilities or whether he has a lazy mentality mixed with a dollar ego.

APME CONTENT COMMITTEE

Most everybody knows by now that a disease which once affected beleaguered politicians has now spread to the press.

We are under siege because of our "credibility gap."

The press, that great bastion of truth and freedom under our American system, is widely suspected of being neither true nor free.

The Content Committee took a plunge into this problem. We sought to spotlight it more than to solve it, and hope we have made an important first step.

Much more is needed, such as:

1. A scientific sampling of public opinion about newspapers which would give editors factual information on which to base corrective programs.

2. Close study of steps taken in various communities to lessen the credibility gap through press councils, newspaper ombudsmen, and the like.

3. Study of the wisdom and practicality of various forms of self-policing by the newspaper profession.

The gap exists; there is no question about it. This is widely acknowledged both by editors and by public officials and leaders replying to a questionnaire of the Content Committee.

The respondents cited such shortcomings as editorial prejudice, half-told stories, inaccurate headlines, and insufficient attention to serious community matters.

The survey, which drew responses from 28 editors and 25 public officials (some of them high in government) was conducted by Courtney R. Sheldon of the *Christian Science Monitor.*

Excerpts from Sheldon's complete report appear separately as part of this committee report.

Youth Looks at Our Newspapers

Under Rene Cazenave of the San Francisco *Examiner,* two questionnaires on how youth views the press drew replies from 110 college students and 87 high school students.

The college students were from 82 colleges and universities in 34 states, and their average age was 21. The high school students represented 75 schools in 27 states, with an average age of 16½.

Some of the students were studying journalism; more were probably not. Cazenave prepared two questionnaires—one for college students and one for high school students—and sent three questionnaires each to a number of managing editors over the country. The managing editors turned them over to students in any way they wished, and the students returned them directly to Cazenave.

Like their elders in Sheldon's survey, the college students reported that newspapers are both unfair and inaccurate in handling many stories.

But in general, they found newspapers fairer and more accurate than television news, news magazines, or radio news.

They found newspapers less interesting than television news or news magazines, but more interesting than radio news. The figures:

	Most accurate	Most fair	Most interesting
Newspapers	35.8%	53.5%	21.5%
Television news	25.5	21.2	36.5
News magazines	32.0	13.1	35.5
Radio news	6.6	12.2	6.5

The high school students, who were asked about interest but not about fairness and accuracy, rated newspapers No. 1:

	Most interesting
Newspapers	31.2%
Television news	30.2
News magazines	28.2
Radio news	10.4

The collegians, asked to volunteer what subjects they felt were handled inaccurately and unfairly by newspapers, cited these (in order):

Inaccurate	Unfair
Campus unrest	Campus unrest
Demonstrations and riots	Negro news
Negro and ghetto problems	National politics
Vietnam	Vietnam
National politics	Urban social problems
Crime news	Youth involvement in crime and protest
Law and order	General crime news

The fairness question was put more specifically to the high school students. "Are newspapers treating teen-agers fairly? Unfairly? What are newspapers not printing about youth that you would like to see?" were the queries.

Many of the teen-agers said newspapers overemphasize negative teen news; do not give sufficient attention to what the good kids are doing; do not report on the causes, but stress the results, of teen crime and violence. A large number said newspapers *do* treat teen unrest *fairly,* however.

Cazenave found that both college students and high school students spend many more hours per week with newspapers than with the other news media:

	College	High School
Newspapers	6 hr., 55 min.	3 hr., 11 min.
Television news	3 hr., 19 min.	2 hr., 32 min.
News magazines	3 hr., 5 min.	1 hr., 15 min.
Radio news	2 hr., 57 min.	2 hr., 41 min.

The young people were asked to volunteer what kind of newspaper news, or what part of the paper, interests them most. The replies, in order:

College	High School
Page One	National news
Local news	Local news
Foreign news	Comics
Sports	World News
Editorials	Sports
Lively arts	Theater and movies
Politics	Politics
Vietnam	Editorials
Social unrest	Humor columns
Comics	School news

What kind of news would the college students like to see more of in the paper? And what would they like to see less of? (Both lists are their own choices, in order.)

More	Less
Racial problems	Crime and murder
Social problems	Society
Politics	College unrest
Campus unrest	Sports
Positive college news	Racial unrest
In-depth analysis of governmental news	Scandal and gossip
	Vietnam
Education	Advice to the lovelorn
Housing and environmental problems	Obituaries
	Traffic accidents
Career opportunities	
Science	
Sex	
Fashion and beauty	

The collegians were also asked to volunteer what they liked most and least about newspapers in general. Their replies:

Most	Least
Variety of content	Too little in-depth reporting and news behind the news
Comprehensive coverage of the news	Slanted news stories
Quick source of information	Playing up "policy" stories and burying others
Depth reporting of news given too briefly on radio and TV	Failure to report controversial subjects impartially
Interpretation, analysis, and editorial views	Sensationalism
Permanent record and reference	Poor headlines
Can be read when convenient	"Bad," "gutless," or "dishonest" editorials
	Meaningless society news and society gossip columns

High school students, completing a more detailed questionnaire than the college students, were asked such questions as these:

Q.: What sports do you like to read about most?
A. (*in order*): High school and college; pro football; pro baseball; pro basketball; auto racing; winter sports; soccer; hockey; wrestling; boxing.
Q. (*for girls*): What sort of "girl-interest" news interests you most (suggesting, as examples, fashion, school news, beauty hints, patterns, society, advice columns, etc.)?
A. (*in order*): Advice columns (Ann Landers and Dear Abby, mostly), fashion, beauty, school news, society, food and recipes, health advice, etiquette, patterns.
Q.: What special columns do you prefer (suggesting science, medicine, war, comment on world and national affairs, humor, entertainment, man-about-town, etc.)?
A. (*in order*): Satire (Buchwald, Hoppe), local columnists, humor, science, medicine, man-about-town, local movies and entertainment, national affairs, world affairs, personalities in the news.

Other questions brought out a hunger among the teen-agers for more information about careers; how to prepare for college; tuition and residence rates at area colleges; what small colleges are like and what colleges are best for certain goals.

Asked about teen columns and teen sections in their local papers, about half reported their papers did not have them. Those who did have them had varied evaluations. In general, the students were quite critical.

Some of their comments:

"I ignore it—the grapevine is newsier."
"Better if it concentrated on local teens—too much 'foreign' stuff."
"Just about our school—wish it had other kids over the country."

"Ridiculous—done by adults who think they know what's 'in'."

"Don't like weekly page. Better if they printed some of it every day."

"Should be a column by some teen every week, writing a piece on anything he likes."

"Too much scholarships and music. Want more on dances, car rallies, rock festivals, styles, things to do, hair styling, fashions and makeup."

Back to the college students. Some of their more interesting comments were these:

"Print more letters to the editor, pictures, world news and less sensationalism"—Houston U. graduate student, 27.

"Go out of your way to show that majority are not long-haired or protesting; encourage creative writers; attack pornography and consumer fleecing"—U.C. Santa Cruz sophomore, 20.

"Dedicate paper to social justice and display effectively without bias"—Colorado College senior, 20.

"Don't overplay crime, accidents on page 1. Stories need more emotional treatment—but backed by facts. Crime or tragedy inside, please"—Oklahoma U. sophomore, 19.

"Hire writers representing both sides (young-old) (black-white) (GOP-Dem.)"—No. Carolina State graduate student, 23.

"Keep the opinions in the editorial page. I'm more interested in accurate reporting than a pretty newspaper"—Wisconsin U. graduate student, 23.

"De-emphasize society news. Report blacks, Puerto Ricans, poor, school people; pay less respect to power structure; give more citizen viewpoints"—Northwestern U. senior, 21.

"Put something in to make them feel good rather than depressed. There are good happenings"—Ashland College junior, 21.

The most insistent and repeated request from both categories of youth questioned was for more in-depth reporting of significant news events and a consistent policy of interpreting the background and meaning of those happenings.

Do Newspapers Have a Serious Credibility Gap?
(*by Courtney R. Sheldon*)

The conclusion seems unavoidable that American newspapers have a credibility gap of substantial proportions.

An impressive preponderance of both editors and public officials or leaders selected as the "major" or "substantial" reasons for public distrust of newspapers such serious shortcomings as:

1. Editorial prejudice shown by placement of stories, size of headlines, unbalanced story content, and length of stories, particularly in coverage of political events.
2. Half-told stories resulting from lax standards for reportorial research and backgrounding of news stories.
3. Too succinct, imprecise, misleading, or inaccurate headlines.
4. Overattention to sensational news of violence and insufficient attention to serious news of community-wide consequence.

Among the critical comments from public officials and leaders were:

Senator George Aiken of Vermont: "Newspapers need to develop more depth in their news accounts and sometimes forget the pressure of the deadline which often leads to inaccurate stories. . . . Newspapers should police themselves just as the American people are demanding the Congress police itself. Wrong doings in the press should be made public."

Fred Harrington, president of the University of Wisconsin: "There is too much this-moment news. To round it out, newspapers add the think-piece. . . . But what is needed more is . . . . a broader story [the interpretation] right in the news story."

Representative John E. Moss of California: "I have no doubt that the public regards many newspapers as biased in their reporting, as dedicated to the making of money, and as committed to causes which are not always identifiable to the public interest. . . ."

Representative Edith Green of Oregon: "While high standards must be expected and required of public-office holders—there is a tendency for some papers to constantly infer that all government people are lazy or greedy or corrupt."

William Tolley, president of Syracuse University: Overattention given to some "insignificant campus disturbances . . . tends to make them contagious."

Among the less critical comments were those of Senator Mike Mansfield of Montana who said that it was not necessary for newspapers to change their concept of news, though "perhaps an adjustment in priorities" is called for.

His Eminence, Richard Cardinal Cushing of Boston observed: "In general I have the impression that the press is doing a good job in presenting the news. There are occasional lapses, the most notable being, in my judgment, the urge to sensationalize, or overdramatize one aspect of a story. I have noticed this especially in the last few years in religious news reporting—which, in general, has improved lately."

89 percent of the public officials and leaders responding to the six-page questionnaire agreed that the APME or one of the other existing professional journalism organizations should set up permanent ethics committees, national or regional, with resources to investigate instances of press misconduct and publicize their findings. (This recommendation was not concurred in by editors, 62 percent of whom were opposed to ethics committees. A typical response was: "It is doubtful it would work. The American Bar Association and the American Medical Association have not been notably successful in self-policing.")

71 percent of the public officials and leaders said

newspapers should establish a special office or staff to investigate public complaints about the newspaper and give the complainer a full report. (54 percent of the editors agreed on the advisability of establishing such a special office. The remaining editors said they preferred to answer complaints through existing channels.)

54 percent of the editors said it would be desirable for the newspapers or professional organizations to finance journalism schools or a public opinion survey group in a countrywide survey of reader opinion on what they trust and distrust in newspapers.

77 percent of the public officials and leaders favored the establishing of local press councils in which representatives of the community regularly meet with their local publisher to open up avenues of discourse on press-community relations. (Newsmen were equally divided on this question, with a number of those who favored it pointing out that the publisher would not be the best one to participate for the newspaper.)

55 percent of the public officials and leaders said "yes" to the question: "Do you feel that attitudes or policies of publishers seriously impair the efforts of editors and writers to achieve greater credibility?" (50 percent of the editors answered similarly, most of them with the reservation, "in some cases.")

The questionnaire was sent to a representative segment of newspaper editors, senators, representatives, mayors, educators, religious leaders, and other community spokesmen in a variety of fields. Answering it required considerable thought and time for the 28 editors and 25 public officials and leaders who responded. Some high governmental officials asked that they not be quoted.

The first section of the questionnaire tried to determine the extent of the credibility gap today as compared to the past.

40 percent of the editors said that public distrust of newspapers is less than at any time in the last few decades; 13 percent said it is greater than at any time in the last few decades; 40 percent said it is about the same as it has always

been; and 7 percent said there is not enough evidence to estimate.

8 percent of the public officials and leaders said public trust in what is read in newspapers is less than at any time in the history of newspapers in the United States; 8 percent said it is greater than at any time in history; 20 percent said it is less than at any time in the last few decades and another 20 percent said it is greater than at any time in the last few decades; 32 percent said it is about the same as it has always been; and 12 percent said there is not enough evidence to estimate.

Any comfort to newspapers in these statistics is drained away by the fact that the judgment that the gap is "about the same as it has always been" is not a qualitative measurement of the gap.

Following is the list of possible reasons for public distrust printed on the questionnaire and how the editors and public officials and leaders evaluated them:

		Editors	Public
Failure of newspapers to print corrections as often as they should and to display them as prominently as they did the erroneous story.	Major cause	23%	40%
	Substantial cause	40	40
	Little or no cause	37	20
Inaccuracies in elementary facts, names, and places (whether a proofreader's, copyreader's, or reporter's error).	Major cause	56%	10%
	Substantial cause	40	40
	Little or no cause	4	50
Evidence of editorial prejudice by placement of stories in paper, size of headlines, unbalanced story content, and length of stories, particularly in coverage of political events.	Major cause	56%	65%
	Substantial cause	37	35
	Little or no cause	7	0
Half-told or misleading stories resulting from lax standards for reportorial research and backgrounding of news stories.	Major cause	64%	65%
	Substantial cause	18	30
	Little or no cause	18	5

		Editors	Public
Half-told and misleading stories due to the pressure of early deadlines and an insistence that the latest spot news be published.	Major cause	29%	41%
	Substantial cause	37	32
	Little or no cause	34	27
Too succinct, imprecise, misleading, or inaccurate headlines.	Major cause	43%	40%
	Substantial cause	38	52
	Little or no cause	19	8
Failure of newspapers to keep the intellectual level of their content apace with the rise in the educational level of the country.	Major cause	12%	18%
	Substantial cause	23	32
	Little or no cause	65	50
Inexpert reporting in specialized news areas such as education, science, religion, the arts.	Major cause	35%	37%
	Substantial cause	27	23
	Little or no cause	38	40
Too many stories attributed to unnamed sources.	Major cause	12%	36%
	Substantial cause	37	28
	Little or no cause	51	36
Conflicts between what is "seen" on television by viewer and what he reads in the newspaper. Public more readily believes "visual" news.	Major cause	18%	19%
	Substantial cause	29	52
	Little or no cause	53	29
The press is always criticized and attacked during periods when the public is frustrated by the enormity of unsolved problems and this is one of those times.	Major cause	54%	24%
	Substantial cause	23	24
	Little or no cause	23	52
The inability of the reader to distinguish between news stories and the opinion articles of columnists.	Major cause	26%	36%
	Substantial cause	26	48
	Little or no cause	48	16
Ignorance of the public on how news is gathered and processed.	Major cause	29%	10%
	Substantial cause	33	33
	Little or no cause	38	57

		Editors	Public
Influence on newspapers by organized pressure groups and public relations specialists, ranging from student demonstrators to governmental offices.	Major cause	5%	33%
	Substantial cause	44	28
	Little or no cause	51	39
Advertiser influence on newspapers in choice of news and in the proportion of different kinds of news.	Major cause	0%	5%
	Substantial cause	0	30
	Little or no cause	100	65
The policies of newspapers are set and carried out by middle- and upper-income whites, and lower-income and minority groups are slighted or misrepresented.	Major cause	5%	15%
	Substantial cause	53	52
	Little or no cause	42	33
Overattention to sensational news of violence and insufficient attention to serious news of community-wide consequence.	Major cause	9%	75%
	Substantial cause	53	20
	Little or no cause	38	5
A newspaper image which is more commercial than professional, more oriented toward profit than journalistic professionalism.	Major cause	4%	22%
	Substantial cause	28	31
	Little or no cause	68	47
Overaggressive behavior of newsmen and photographers in covering some stories.	Major cause	4%	33%
	Substantial cause	48	38
	Little or no cause	48	29
Violation of the confidence of a news source.	Major cause	6%	10%
	Substantial cause	14	15
	Little or no cause	80	75
Insufficient space devoted to readers' letters, especially those containing views contrary to the paper's editorial opinion.	Major cause	12%	9%
	Substantial cause	23	25
	Little or no cause	65	66

		Editors	Public
Top editors too busy with matters other than the content of their papers.	Major cause	20%	25%
	Substantial cause	27	15
	Little or no cause	53	60
Too much in newspapers about newspapers and newsmen in contrast to news of other professions.	Major cause	4%	0%
	Substantial cause	11	5
	Little or no cause	85	95
A too defensive attitude on the part of the press when it is attacked or criticized.	Major cause	11%	49%
	Substantial cause	39	28
	Little or no cause	50	23
The reluctance of newspapers to stand together and censure specific unethical practices by individual newspapers.	Major cause	16%	32%
	Substantial cause	44	40
	Little or no cause	40	28
Severe competition from other professions for outstanding young talent, resulting in a lowering of journalistic standards to fill jobs.	Major cause	33%	15%
	Substantial cause	37	50
	Little or no cause	30	35

Of particular interest in the above tabulation is that public officials and leaders single out the following as possible causes of public distrust of newspapers much more often than the editors:

Failure to print corrections
Too many unattributed stories
Inability of reader to tell the difference between news stories and columnists
Influence of pressure groups on newspapers
Overattention to sensational news of violence
The profit-making image of newspapers
Overaggressive behavior of newsmen and photographers
A too-defensive attitude on the part of the press when it is attacked

Possible causes of distrust which editors rated much higher than the public answers were:

Inaccuracies in elementary facts
Press attacked during periods of public frustration

On a question of whether there was any likelihood that public distrust would result in new laws restricting the press and "Would you favor any such restrictions?" 85 percent of the editors said "no" to the former and 100 percent "no" to the latter. The public response was 76 percent "no" to the former and also 100 percent "no" to the latter.

One editor, George R. Kentera, managing editor of the Newark *News*, answered "no" to the first question and then commented: "I base my answer on the increased liberalism of the U.S. Supreme Court in this regard. There will be, however, increasing restraint placed upon newspapers by the courts. Some of this restraint is, and will be, justified; and I foresee the day when some will not, and that day will produce a new case for the Supreme Court."

Senator Margaret Chase Smith of Maine recommended, "Revise our libel laws and court rulings more nearly like those of the English courts."

Should newspapers appoint to their boards of directors one member to represent the public? Editors answered 67 percent "no" and 33 percent "yes"; public, 52 percent "yes" and 48 percent "no."

Editors were asked several additional questions related to any credibility gap, some of which follow:

Are newspaper editorial staffs too small to devote the amount of time needed for thorough research and greater accuracy? 56 percent answered yes.

How practical is it to hire experts in specialized fields, and train them in newspaper writing? 61 percent said not practical or needed and 39 percent said practical in certain areas, such as music, science, medicine.

Are graduates of schools of journalism more helpful than other recruits in preventing a credibility gap with readers? 51

percent said not necessarily; 23 percent said no and 10 percent said yes.

Is the general intelligence level of all journalism recruits higher or lower in recent times? 68 percent said higher, 22 percent same, 10 percent lower.

Appendix F
NEWSPAPERS' USE OF INTERNAL CRITICISM

This is News Research Bulletin No. 9, 3 June 1970, published by the American Newspaper Publishers Association. It is reprinted here with ANPA permission. It includes the description and results of a study conducted by Professor William B. Blankenburg of the University of Wisconsin, which was commissioned by the ANPA News Research Center.

NEWSPAPERS' USE OF INTERNAL CRITICISM

Journalists are often admonished to be critical of their own work. "The need is for constant self-appraisal," said the National Commission on the Causes and Prevention of Violence in its final report. Yet little study has been given the press's own criticism. Speeches and articles that cite "self-improvement" speak mainly of circulation and capital expenditures, and it remains both fair and pertinent to ask journalists how they take stock of themselves.

This study explores the practice of *internal criticism* on daily newspapers—criticism that goes on between and among journalists in the same newsroom.

Internal criticism is one of four kinds of press evaluation that can be distinguished by source. *External criticism* comes from any nonjournalist—a reader, a member of a local press council, or even the vice-president of the United States. *Intramural criticism* arises within the profession and passes between media. The *Chicago Journalism Review*, API seminars, and the proposed ASNE Grievance Committee are vehicles of intramural criticism. *Self-criticism* is a newsman's analysis of his own performance.

In February 1970 questionnaires on internal criticism were mailed to 340 newspaper executives whose names were drawn primarily from the APME membership list. Responses were received from 234 newspapers in 43 states and the District of Columbia, for a return rate of 69 percent. The responding newspapers ranged in size from the El Reno (Okla.) *Tribune* (circulation 4,507) to the New York (N.Y.) *Daily News* (over 2 million). The median size was 50,000. For some of the following analysis, the newspapers are grouped by circulation quintile (i.e., approximately 47 papers in each group) in order to determine whether size affects critical practices. (For example, one might expect larger newspapers to make greater use of impersonal methods—such as bulletin boards—than do smaller newspapers.)

The questionnaire defined criticism as an evaluation of performance that could include praise as well as blame. The respondents—mainly editors—were asked if their newspapers used any of five general methods of internal criticism: critical notes posted on newsroom bulletin boards, memoranda written to individual staffers, an employe publication that carries criticism, conferences with individual staffers to evaluate their work, and group meetings that have some critical content.

What Methods Do They Use?

A three-page questionnaire cannot do full justice to the phenomenon of internal criticism, but the responses do paint a broad-stroke portrait of current practices. Table 1 shows the percentage of newspapers that use each method of criticism at least occasionally and those that use each method with some regularity.

Table 1 **Methods of Internal Criticism**

	Used	Used Regularly
Individual conference	92.7%	43.3%
Group conference	73.5	56.4
Memoranda	74.4	57.4
Bulletin board	53.8	42.9
Employee publication	19.7	—
Mean number of methods used	3.1	

Table 2 (on page 216) shows the differences in usage by circulation size.

Internal criticism appears to be widely practiced. Only two newspapers, with circulations of 5,300 and 46,000, reported no critical activities. The most widely used method, individual conferences, is also the most personal and flexible. There is little variation by size of newspapers regarding this technique. However, the regularity of its use drops sharply among the largest newspapers.

Almost three-fourths of the newspapers conducted group meetings that contained critical content. The smaller newspapers were more likely to have these meetings, but the very largest held them most regularly. Because a meeting can cover a variety of topics, the editors were asked whether criticism was only incidental to other matters. About 58 percent said it was not incidental, and some were quite vehement about its importance.

The less personal methods of conveying criticism—

Table 2 **Methods of Internal Criticism Used by Daily Newspapers of Varying Size**

	Size of Newspapers[a]				
Methods of criticism	Small (4,000–24,999)	Medium–small (25,000–39,999)	Medium (40,000–64,999)	Medium–large (65,000–164,999)	Large (165,000+)
Individual conference					
used	89.8%	95.7%	93.3%	93.6%	91.5%
regularly	40.9	40.9	52.4	54.5	27.9
Group conference					
used	77.6	84.8	68.9	72.3	63.8
regularly	50.0	56.4	51.6	55.9	70.0
Memoranda					
used	69.4	67.4	71.1	89.4	74.5
regularly	58.8	54.8	62.5	59.5	51.4
Bulletin board					
used	48.9	45.7	55.5	57.4	61.7
regularly	45.8	33.3	52.0	40.7	41.4
Employe publication					
used	14.3	10.9	20.0	29.8	23.4
Mean number of methods					
used	3.0	3.0	3.1	3.4	3.1

[a] Approximately 47 newspapers in each size-group.

memoranda and bulletin boards—were more heavily used by larger newspapers. Even so, at least half of the smaller papers employed these techniques. Some editors, however, were appalled at the thought of using bulletin boards for criticism. Several said it was their policy to "praise in public, condemn in private"; hence the attractiveness of individual conferences. (Contrary to stereotype, a great number of editors showed solicitude for reporters' feelings.)

Employe publications were used by about one-fifth of all respondents as a means of criticism. While several editors expressed favor for a *Winners & Sinners* type of publication, many also found its production a considerable chore. About half of the respondents who used a publication said theirs carried words of praise only.

As might be expected, several respondents used additional and more specialized methods than the five shown in the table. Accuracy surveys, suggestion boxes, and internal circulation of a marked copy of the day's issue were among those mentioned.

On the average, the newspapers surveyed used three of the major methods, with little variation by size of newspaper. The "medium-large" papers were the most inclined to use more.

The editors were allowed to define "regular use" as they saw fit. However, they were asked for the frequency of use of four of the methods, and their responses are summarized in table 3.

Table 3 **Frequency of Use of Four Methods of Internal Criticism**

Frequency	Bulletin Board	Memoranda	Individual Conference	Group Conference[a]
Daily	9.2%	12.9%	1.8%	9.7%
Daily to weekly	10.9	1.2	2.7	1.9
Biweekly	17.6	3.5	6.3	25.3
Monthly	2.5	1.2	.9	8.4
Monthly to semi-annually	3.4	1.2	4.5	24.0
Semiannually	0	0	23.4	7.8
Annually	0	2.4	9.0	0
Occasionally or "as needed"	56.3	77.6	62.2	22.7

[a] If more than one kind of conference was cited, the highest frequency was used.

The majority of respondents stated no regular interval for the use of bulletin boards, memoranda, or individual conferences. These methods, which require no elaborate planning, were generally used as the need arose. However, group meetings do present logistical problems, and it is not surprising to find them used less casually. The smaller newspapers were more likely to call meetings "as needed." Larger newspapers reported more daily group meetings—but in the form of executive "news conferences" rather than full-staff or departmental sessions. The 23.4 percent of newspapers that reported semiannual individual conferences typically used them for salary reviews.

Who Directs the Criticism?

The publisher, executive editor, and editor were rarely the sole directors of critical activities (their participation was highest on the smallest newspapers), but they frequently joined with middle-rank executives to provide criticism (see table 4).

Often there was no single leader. A "combination of executives" predominated in the areas of individual conferences, bulletin boards, and memoranda. However, the leadership of staff meetings fell mainly to one person, the managing editor, who, by the way, was the most frequently cited single leader.

Because the critical activities were usually initiated by executives, it may be fair to assume that much of the criticism was one-way, from the top down. Certainly the less personal modes of criticism—bulletin boards, memos, and company publications—are inherently unilateral. Several of the editors' comments support this assumption. An executive of a leading eastern daily said, "I cannot believe that working journalists from several levels can meet as 'equal' professionals because their responsibilities are far from equal."

However, conferences do provide an opportunity for dialogue, and although executives usually lead the discussions, 35 percent of those who used group conferences

Table 4 **Leadership of Internal Criticism: Percent of Respondents Citing Leaders of Each Critical Activity**

Critical Activity

Source or Director	Bulletin Boards	Memoranda	Company Publication	Individual Conference	Group Conference
Publisher	.8%	2.9%	2.2%	1.4%	2.9%
Executive editor	4.9	4.6	2.2	2.3	5.8
Editor	4.1	5.2	10.9	3.7	13.4
Managing editor	31.9	27.2	13.0	24.7	39.5
Other news executive[a]	9.8	9.2	43.5	22.3	11.0
Combination of Executives	42.6	50.3	19.6	45.6	26.7
Other[b]	5.7	.6	8.7	0	.6

[a] Most often the city editor or his assistant.

[b] Noneditorial sources, including personnel managers, outside experts, and readers.

did mention that they sought topics or feedback from junior editors or reporters.

Individual conferences may be less egalitarian than group meetings. The majority of editors (65.6 percent) said the former were called because of a reporter's performance—usually bad performance. (One-fifth said the meetings were part of a regular pay review.) Still, some crosstalk is possible, as Warren R. Gardner, editor of the Meriden (Conn.) *Morning Record* indicated: "Beginners are counseled frequently, and we point out how they may improve their work. It's a dialogue in which they are invited to ask questions about whatever they want to know about their work or the paper."

There is a sufficient variety of conferences to make an evaluation of equality hazardous. Forty percent of the editors used more than one kind of group meeting (e.g., full staff, executives-only, or departmental), and as might be expected, the smaller newspapers made more use of full-staff meetings while the larger papers turned more to specialized groups. Table 5 shows a pattern of usage of multiple meetings.

Table 5 **Percentage of Newspapers Using More Than One Kind of Group Meeting**

All	Small	Medium–Small	Medium	Medium–Large	Large
43.7%	25.0%	34.8%	74.0%	50.0%	38.5%

It may be that the medium-sized newspapers are at a point where it is both necessary and desirable to use a variety of meetings. Smaller newspapers can assemble the full staff with relative ease, and larger newspapers must make do with departmental or executive meetings.

Are They Satisfied with What They Are Doing?

The editors were asked to evaluate their present methods of internal criticism, and their answers suggest that they are generally satisfied. Only one of the 234 respondents said that his newspaper's methods were "not very valuable." Twenty-eight percent held their criticism to be "highly valuable"; 56 percent assessed theirs as "quite valuable"; and 16 percent felt theirs was of "uncertain value." Little variation was apparent by size of newspaper. The largest newspapers expressed the highest satisfaction, but the difference is not significant.

The editors were also asked for "ideal" ways to conduct internal criticism. Here too they indicated some satisfaction: their most frequent first choice was to refine their present practices. Table 6 summarizes these responses.

More face-to-face criticism, by means of both individual and group conferences, was generally desired. The smallest newspapers were the least inclined to stick with their present methods and most desirous of additional group meetings. Metropolitan editors were not inclined to add more meetings, but did show interest in designating a "house critic." The use of a newsroom publication like the *New York Times' Winners & Sinners* was a frequent collateral choice.

Table 6 **How Can Internal Criticism Be Improved? (Percent of First Choices)**

	All	Small	Medium–Small	Medium	Medium–Large	Large
Refine present methods	28.7%	12.5%	40.0%	24.1%	38.7%	29.0%
Have more individual conferences	24.8	25.0	23.3	37.9	12.9	25.8
Add regular group conferences	20.3	43.7	16.7	24.1	6.5	9.7
Add full-time critic or supervisor	9.8	6.3	3.3	0	19.4	19.4
Use *Winners & Sinners* publication	7.8	3.1	3.3	3.4	12.9	6.5
Use outside consultant	2.6	3.1	3.3	0	6.5	0
Seek more staff participation in criticism	2.6	3.1	3.3	3.4	0	3.2
Other[a]	3.9	3.1	0	6.9	3.2	6.5

[a] For example, marked copies and suggestion boxes.

Some Notes on Quality and Quantity

The picture that emerges is one of extensive critical activity, with virtually every participating newspaper reporting the use of at least one method of self-examination. Much of the criticism is conveyed personally on an "as-needed" basis by various hands in middle management. The editors were generally pleased with what they were doing, but saw room for improvement.

Yet while the quantity of internal criticism is extensive, its quality is less certain. It is not even clear that internal criticism is altogether virtuous. Some executives may regard it as harmful to a team spirit. Some reporters may view it as a thumbscrew to enforce "policy." Insensitively applied, internal criticism may be a tool of what editor Edward T.

Fairchild of the Athol (Mass.) *Daily News* deplores as "factory management in news departments."

Some comments from the respondents reveal problems with internal criticism:

"We've found that daily staff news conferences, or weekly or monthly staff conferences, produce little of value and generate little staff interest," wrote Jerry Schniepp, managing editor of the Springfield (Ill.) *State Register*.

"Too often discussions can bog down on extraneous comment—excuses for doing this or that," said E. Curtiss Pierson, managing editor of New London (Conn.) *Day*. A southern executive editor said that group discussions were "too often dominated by the gabby."

Another major problem was noted by a midwestern editor: "Reporters (editors, too) are very sensitive to criticism, often resent it thoroughly. Their attitude often is, 'Nobody could have done it any better, considering the poor info available and the pressure of deadlines.' "

Despite its difficulties, internal criticism seems necessary to most editors. "The hardest part of internal criticism is to get across to the editorial employes that it's a natural part of the operation," wrote Bruce H. McIntyre, managing editor of the Battle Creek (Mich.) *Enquirer* and *News*. A Georgia editor agreed: "It sometimes gets a little rough, but it does clear the air."

Internal criticisms may also be needed because times change: "Our discussions are based on a recognition that newspaper policies and procedures that formerly were acceptable may no longer be right," wrote Arthur Gallagher, editor of the Ann Arbor (Mich.) *News*.

Donald Johnson, managing editor of the Niagara Falls (N.Y.) *Gazette*, added: "We find that seldom is a specific problem unrelated to other things which need discussion and possible change. This often leads into other departments and long-term habits and patterns which need revision. We frequently find that problems have been 'caused' by very real pressures from other sources than editors had imagined and that misunderstandings about process and policies can arise almost spontaneously."

Though some workers resent criticism, others may seek it. "I think a staffer is interested in knowing that his supervisors follow his work closely and I think he generally appreciates criticism—even unfavorable criticism. A frequent complaint I get from young staffers is that 'nobody talks to me about how I'm doing. Am I cutting it or not?' This is a damning indictment of us, and I hope we can do better," wrote Darrell Sifford, managing editor of the Charlotte (N.C.) *News.*

These and other responses suggest to the author that any editor who wishes to review his newspaper's internal criticism should consider these qualities:

Six Qualities of Internal Criticism

1. Even-handedness. Among the major journalistic issues of the 1970s will be the staff's role in policy making and a reporter's autonomy. Internal criticism that invites an easy give-and-take may help resolve those issues with minimum acrimony. Kurt Luedtke, assistant to the executive editor of the Detroit (Mich.) *Free Press,* warned: "Most newspaper managements see internal criticism as marching down a one-way street—from the owners to the continually erring staffers. That sort of criticism is almost useless and potentially destructive. Neither do most publishers and executive editors want to hear what's wrong from the staff."

This study took no direct measure of authoritarianism, but as noted earlier, many respondents professed to be solicitous of staff viewpoints. But some quickly raised the defense of "the right to manage," and one managing editor said he liked to "call 'em over to my office and give 'em hell."

An editor can, of course, err on the side of chumminess. The managing editor of a midwestern metro, after lamenting his distance from reporters, put it this way: "I try to mix with staff members outside the office—the danger, and my caution, is that I don't intrude on their bitch sessions, and that I don't appear to be trying to make a pal out of myself."

2. Regularity without Regimentation. High among the

editors' desires for improving criticism was a wish for a fair degree of regularity, especially for staff meetings. Several editors confessed that conferences were often skipped under pressure of time.

It follows that if criticism is important, it should be done systematically—but a nice judgment must be made. One leading southern daily takes pride in its semiannual, four-page, company-wide employe evaluation forms. Perhaps this pride is misplaced; an Ohio editor finds this sort of analysis "too much like the damned army."

3. Significance. Much individual criticism treats practical problems of style and accuracy. Several editors expressed concern that such day-to-day issues can bog down staff meetings, which, if they are worth calling, should cope with more far-reaching matters. One trouble with his meetings, reported John H. McMillan, managing editor of the Worcester (Mass.) *Telegram,* is that "too much time and attention is devoted to design and makeup and not enough to content." And, he added, "There is the reluctance of almost everyone over thirty to be frank."

It may also be wise to consider whether individual criticism should always be shot from the hip. An Illinois editor observed, "Criticism should be made on the basis of a week's performance by a reporter, thereby eliminating the one-day explanations (legitimate ones), like 'not feeling well,' and thereby getting a more balanced picture." Murray B. Light of the Buffalo (N.Y.) *News* suggested that "personal communication with staff members of a more formal nature than an across-the-desk relationship is often helpful. Conferences set up by appointment give the staffer the feeling that his particular problem has been given consideration in advance."

4. Priority relates to significance and regularity. A striking example came from a 15,000-circulation Nebraska daily whose editor wrote, "Our staff meetings are informal, but everyone is to attend unless excused. Nobody leaves to answer the phone or take care of walk-in news sources except in case of emergency. A part-timer courteously handles calls, offering call-backs."

Many editors suggested that the best criticism is that which catches errors before they get into print and corrects poor performance before it becomes ingrained. This sort of precedence implies added manpower and easy access between staffers—and not always from the top down. On the Tampa (Fla.) *Times*, according to managing editor H. Doyle Harvill, "There is complete freedom of access to the managing editor at all times—often meetings with outsiders are interrupted by staff writers."

5. Reference and Review. One way to prevent group conferences from wandering is to provide agendas and reference material. "At evening meetings, topics are picked in advance so we don't drink too much of the host's beer," wrote Paul J. Day of the Middleton (Ohio) *Journal*. But only 9 percent of the respondents who used group conferences employed agendas.

If meetings treat significant topics, perhaps some record should be made of the discussion, although only 18 percent reported keeping notes. Joel D. Smyth, managing editor of the Delaware *State News* in Dover, has saved tape recordings of some staff discussions (as on libel) for the instruction of new reporters.

Relatedly, some editors keep copies of critical memoranda in order to review the effectiveness of their criticism.

6. Flexibility. Critical methods can be used in widely varying combinations, and many editors stressed the value of informality and showed some willingness to experiment.

Not all experiments work: The Ansonia (Conn.) *Sentinel* tried a "two-city-editor" solution to the problem of freeing one man to work closely with reporters, but this technique proved too expensive in manpower for a small (17,500) newspaper. Some larger papers, like the Toledo (Ohio) *Blade*, do have an assistant city editor in charge of training, and smaller dailies sometimes engage outside experts for seminars, as the Reno (Nev.) *Gazette* did with typographer Edmund Arnold.

The idea of coupling outside expertise to internal criticism is attractive to many editors. A major midwestern daily has commissioned a retired journalism professor to write critical memoranda, and a Texas daily circulates the criticism of a highly experienced nonsupervisor whose name is kept secret from the staff.

But many executives would agree with Warren Lerude of Reno, who noted, "Really, we are quite expert in knowing our shortcomings and the best criticism can be offered by ourselves to ourselves since we are closest to our problems." Still, newsmen may be too close, and, like James P. Brown of The Saginaw (Mich.) *News*, may wish to use such tools as the Brinton-Bush-Newell questionnaire of audience attitudes, which he administered to employees. Several newspapers also conduct regular accuracy surveys, picking several stories at random each day and asking the newsmakers whether the reports were accurate.

Group conferences can range in style from a rump session around the city desk to a complete hiatus from the city. The Hutchinson (Kan.) *News* occasionally holds seminars away from the shop, and a large midwestern daily has semiannual discussions for key editors at a nearby hotel. Once a year the small (5,475) Camarillo (Calif.) *Daily News* takes its entire news staff into Los Angeles for an all-day seminar, often with a visiting expert.

Few newspapers can free the staff all at one time. Henry McLeod, managing editor of the Seattle (Wash.) *Times*, reported a partial solution: "Every five or six weeks we have two staff meetings on successive afternoons. They are open to any staffer who wants to sign up, and are held from 3:30 to 5:30 or 6:00 P.M. The managing editor always attends. These are completely open, and staffers analyze coverage of various stories or subjects, criticize or inquire about the paper's policy. . . . The assistant city editor writes a detailed report of the meetings and posts it on the office bulletin board for those who were unable to attend."

How Much Internal Criticism Is Enough?

William A. Draves, managing editor of the Fond du Lac (Wis.) *Commonwealth Reporter*, described his use of bulletin boards, marked copies, weekly conferences with cubs and interns, six-month reviews with experienced reporters, monthly executive conferences, and occasional full-staff meetings. Then he mused, "I wonder if other papers do as little as we apparently do with internal criticism."

An Indiana editor had fewer doubts (and hardly any internal criticism): "If we had all that time we would use it to improve our news coverage and reporting. We are not in the ivory tower, but down at the grass roots."

Edwin M. Miller of the Portland (Ore.) *Oregonian* agreed that "there is always the problem of having so many meetings that the work doesn't get done." But he wished for more group conferences in his own shop, and added, "A managing editor could, with profit to his paper, schedule a once-a-week discussion with various members of the staff. Some meetings would be with sports, or women's, or general assignment people. Other meetings could be more general."

In sum, the responses demonstrate that much can be done with internal criticism, despite powerful constraints of time and manpower. An appropriate mix of critical methods, and an evaluation of their worth, must be determined primarily within each newspaper by both the givers and receivers of criticism—whose roles should be occasionally swapped.

As Kurt Luedtke of the Detroit (Mich.) *Free Press* observed, "It's worth noting that staff criticism, comment, and participation at a healthy newspaper should be part of the ongoing process, part of the fabric of a newspaper."

NOTES

Chapter 1. Power, the Press, and Criticism

1. Walter Lippmann, *The Public Philosophy* (New York: Mentor, 1955), p. 128.
2. Charles R. Wright, *Mass Communication* (New York: Random House, 1959), pp. 16–23.
3. Commission on Freedom of the Press, *A Free and Responsible Press* (Chicago: University of Chicago Press, 1947), pp. 20–28.
4. Lippmann, *The Public Philosophy*, p. 40.
5. "Judging the Fourth Estate: A *Time*-Louis Harris Poll," *Time*, 5 September 1968, p. 38.
6. Ibid.
7. M. L. Stein, "The Press Under Assault: View from the U.S.," *Saturday Review*, 12 October 1968, p. 75.
8. Norman E. Isaacs, "Agnew, the National Mood and the Media," *ASNE Bulletin*, no. 537 (January 1970): 2.
9. Northrop Frye, *Anatomy of Criticism* (New York: Atheneum, 1969), p. 11.

10. Ibid., p. 5.
11. Ibid., p. 4.
12. Louis M. Lyons, "Liebling, Libel, and the Press," *Atlantic*, May 1964, p. 46.
13. Robert J. Manning, "Journalism and Foreign Affairs," in *The Responsibility of the Press*, ed. Gerald Gross (New York: Simon & Schuster, 1966), pp. 193–94.
14. Isaacs, "Agnew and the Media," p. 1.
15. Hugh Dalziel Duncan, *Language and Literature in Society* (Chicago: University of Chicago Press, 1953), p. 65.
16. Ibid., pp. 61–62.
17. Ibid., p. 60.
18. T. S. Eliot, *To Criticize the Critic, and Other Writings* (New York: Farrar, Straus & Giroux, 1965), pp. 11–14.
19. Ibid., p. 21.
20. Herbert Brucker, "A Conscience for the Press," *Saturday Review*, 9 May 1970, p. 60.
21. Charles C. Clayton, "Enforceable Code of Ethics," *Grassroots Editor* 10, no. 4 (July–August 1969): 18.
22. W. H. Ferry and Harry S. Ashmore, "Mass Communications," an occasional paper of the Center for the Study of Democratic Institutions (1966), p. 38.
23. Arthur E. Rowse et al., "Hutchins Commission: Responses," *Columbia Journalism Review* 5, no. 3 (Fall 1967): 53–54.
24. W. H. Werkmeister, *Theories of Ethics* (Lincoln, Neb.: Johnsen Publishing Co., 1961), p. 7.
25. Brucker, "Conscience for the Press," p. 61.
26. Sylvan Meyer, "I Think Mr. McLuhan Is Trying to Tell Us Something," *Nieman Reports* 23, no. 2 (June 1969): 10.

Chapter 2. The Fabric of Press Criticism: Unbroken Threads

1. *True Briton*, 19 July 1723.
2. Willard G. Bleyer, *Main Currents in the History of American Journalism* (Boston: Houghton Mifflin, 1927), p. 33.
3. *Gazette of the United States*, 4 March 1799.
4. *Farmer's Museum, or Lay Preacher's Gazette*, 14 April 1799.
5. *Daily Advertiser*, 7 April 1814.
6. Boston *Spectator*, 18 October 1836.
7. John Tebbel, *The Compact History of the American Newspaper* (New York: Hawthorn Books, 1963), p. 99.

8. Frank L. Mott, *American Journalism* (New York: Macmillan, 1962), p. 311.
9. *Montana Journalism Review*, no. 13 (1970): 32.
10. *Springfield Weekly Republican*, 20 December 1872.
11. Bleyer, *Main Currents*, p. 287.
12. Ibid., p. 288.
13. Edwin Emery and Henry L. Smith, *The Press and America* (Englewood Cliffs, N.J.: Prentice-Hall, 1959), p. 445.
14. Nelson A. Crawford, *The Ethics of Journalism* (New York: Alfred A. Knopf, 1924), p. 42.
15. Ibid., pp. 39–182.
16. Upton Sinclair, *The Brass Check* (Pasadena, Calif.: privately published, 1919), p. 436.
17. Ibid., p. 404.
18. Nelson A. Crawford, *The Ethics of Journalism* (New York: Alfred A. Knopf, 1924), pp. 202 ff.
19. Emery and Smith, *Press and America*, p. 478.
20. Crawford, Ethics, pp. 202 ff.
21. Ibid., p. 164.
22. Ibid., pp. 202 ff.
23. Ibid., pp. 235–36.
24. Randy Block, "How Effective Is Our Code of Ethics," *ASNE Bulletin*, no. 521 (July 1968): 2–3, 13.
25. Linda Wiener Hausman, "Criticism of the Press in U.S. Periodicals, 1900–1939: An Annotated Bibliography," *Journalism Monographs*, no. 4 (August 1967).
26. Ibid.
27. G. Edward Gerald, *The Social Responsibility of the Press* (Minneapolis: University of Minnesota Press, 1964), p. 50.
28. Ibid.
29. As quoted by Richard W. Lee, *History of the Newspaper Association Managers, Inc.,* (Denver: Big Mountain Press, 1967), p. 78.
30. George Seldes, *Freedom of the Press* (Garden City, N.Y.: Garden City Publishing, 1937), p. 367.
31. Bruce Bliven, "Balance Sheet of American Journalism," *New Republic*, 10 March 1941, pp. 331–34.
32. George L. Bird and Frederic E. Merwin, eds., *The Newspaper and Society* (New York: Prentice-Hall, 1942), p. 395.
33. Mott, *American Journalism*, p. 763.
34. Ibid., p. 758.
35. Ibid., p. 759.
36. Commission on Freedom of the Press, *A Free and Responsible Press* (Chicago: University of Chicago Press, 1947), p. 68.

37. As quoted by William C. Sexton, "Education for Journalism . . . the Second Century," *Quill* 57, no. 2 (February 1969): 14.
38. Charles C. Wright, *Mass Communications: A Sociological Perspective* (New York: Random House, 1959), p. 91.
39. Leo Rosten, "The Intellectual and the Mass Media: Some Rigorously Random Remarks," *Daedalus* 99, no. 2 (Spring 1960): 333.
40. Ibid., pp. 333–46.
41. "What's Wrong with the Press?," *Newsweek*, 29 November 1965, p. 58.
42. Ibid.
43. Lester Markel, "The Real Sins of the Press," *Harper's*, December 1962, pp. 86–87, 92–93.
44. "Ethics and the Press: Conflicts of Interest, Pressures Still Distort Some Papers' Coverage," *Wall Street Journal*, 25 July 1967, p. 1.
45. J. Edward Murray, "The Image of the Newspapers," speech given at the Associated Press Managing Editors Convention, San Diego, Calif., November 18, 1966.
46. Ibid., pp. 9–13.
47. A. H. Raskin, "What's Wrong with American Newspapers," *New York Times Magazine*, 11 June 1967, p. 28.
48. Ibid.
49. Ibid., p. 84.
50. Peter B. Clark, "The Reporter and the Power Structure," *Nieman Reports* 23, no. 1 (March 1969): 60.
51. Ibid., pp. 11–13.
52. Spiro Agnew, text of speech, Philadelphia *Evening Bulletin*, 14 November 1969.
53. Ibid.

Chapter 3. The Anatomy of Press Criticism: Conduct and Nature

1. Carle Hodge, "A Wayward Pressman Becomes a Critic," *Editor & Publisher*, 14 August 1948, p. 10.
2. As quoted by J. Anthony Lukas, "Taking Our Cue From Joe," [*More*] 2, no. 5 (May 1972): 18.
3. Ibid., p. 20.
4. A. J. Liebling, "The Rubber-Type Army," in *Problems of Journalism—1951: Proceedings of the 1951 Convention of the American Society of Newspaper Editors* (Washington, D.C.: 1951), p. 225.
5. A. J. Liebling, *The Sweet Science* (New York: Viking Press, 1956), p. 6.

6. *Columbia Journalism Review* 6, no. 3 (Fall 1967): 30–31.
7. Anonymous, *Columbia Journalism Review* 11, no. 4 (November/December 1972): 7.
8. Washington *Post*, 1 October 1972.
9. Edmund M. Midura, "An Evaluation of A. J. Liebling's Performance as a Critic of the Press" (Ph.D. Dissertation, School of Journalism, University of Iowa, 1968), p. 4.
10. Louis M. Lyons, *Reporting the News* (New York: Atheneum, 1968), p. 2.
11. Midura, "Liebling," p. 5.
12. Anonymous, *Time*, 6 December 1971, p. 74.
13. Ibid.
14. Ibid.
15. Anonymous, "Advisory Council," *Editor & Publisher*, 28 July 1951, p. 36.
16. As quoted by Robert U. Brown, "Press Council Established," *Editor & Publisher*, 24 February 1973, p. 40.
17. Nelson A. Crawford, *The Ethics of Journalism* (New York: Alfred A. Knopf, 1924), pp. 202 ff.
18. Anonymous, "Ex-C.E. Relishes Diplomatic Post: The Readers' Man," *Editor & Publisher*, 5 February 1972, p. 30.
19. Keith P. Sanders, "What Are Daily Newspapers Doing to Be Responsive to Readers' Criticisms: A Survey of U.S. Daily Newspaper Accountability Systems," News Research Bulletin No. 9, American Newspaper Publishers Association, 30 November 1973, p. 67.
20. Judge Harold R. Medina was chairman of the Fair Trial Committee of the Association of the Bar of the City of New York. The committee found that the constitutional "guarantee of free speech and free press, and the critical importance of the concept of freedom of communication that underlies this guarantee, preclude, on both constitutional and policy grounds, direct controls of the news media by a governmental scheme of legislative or judicial regulation." Medina suggested that the judicial establishment "put its own house in order." See: Robert G. Gichenberg, "The Price of Liberty," *Albany Law Review* 32, no. 2 (Winter 1968): 324.
21. Anonymous, "ASNE Officials Comment on Medina Report," *ASNE Bulletin*, no. 507 (April 1967): 5.
22. William L. Rivers, "The Dinosaur and His Critics," in *Backtalk*, ed. William L. Rivers, William B. Blankenburg, Kenneth Starck,

Earl Reeves (San Francisco: Canfield Press, 1972), p. 16.

Chapter 4. The National Press Council: From FDR to Xanadu?

1. Alfred McClung Lee, *The Daily Newspaper in America* (New York: Macmillan, 1947), p. 245.
2. Ibid., p. 243.
3. E. F. Tomkins, ed., *Selections from the Writings and Speeches of William Randolph Hearst* (San Francisco: privately published, 1948), pp. 334–35.
4. Robert M. Hutchins et al., *A Free and Responsible Press* (Chicago: University of Chicago Press, 1947), p. 100.
5. Harry S. Ashmore, "Cause, Effect, and Cure," *Mass Communications*, occasional paper of the Center for the Study of Democratic Institutions of the Fund for the Republic, Inc. (1966), p. 33.
6. As cited by *Columbia Journalism Review* 11, no. 6 (March/April 1973): 57.
7. Ibid.
8. Ibid.
9. Robert U. Brown, "National Press Council," *Editor & Publisher*, 20 January 1973, p. 52.
10. Ibid.
11. Barry Bingham, Sr., et al., *A Free and Responsive Press* (New York: Twentieth Century Fund, 1973), pp. 6–8.
12. Ibid., p. 8.
13. Hutchins, *A Free and Responsible Press*, p. 100.
14. Ibid., pp. 100–102.
15. Ibid., p. 1.
16. Bingham, *A Free and Responsive Press*, p. 5.
17. William L. Rivers in "Prescription for the Press," in *Backtalk*, ed. William L. Rivers, William B. Blankenburg, Kenneth Starck, Earl Reeves (San Francisco: Canfield Press, 1972), p. 126.
18. Ibid., p. 12.
19. Council on Research, "A Plan for the Evaluation of Communication Agencies," *Journalism Quarterly* 25, no. 4 (December 1948): 396.
20. Ralph O. Nafziger, "Official Minutes of the 1967 Convention,

Association for Education in Journalism," *Journalism Quarterly*
44, no. 4 (Winter 1967): 799.

Chapter 5. Epilogue and Orwell

1. Justice Felix Frankfurter, Dennis v. United States, 341 U.S. 549
   (1951).
2. Morris L. Ernst, in the introduction to *The First Freedom*, ed.
   Bryce W. Rucker (Carbondale: University of Illinois Press, 1968),
   p. xvii.
3. Robert M. Hutchins et al., *A Free and Responsible Press*
   (Chicago: University of Chicago Press, 1947), p. 80.
4. *Newsweek*, 10 December 1973, p. 45.
5. Ibid.

SELECTED
BIBLIOGRAPHY

Books

Bagdikian, Ben. *Some Effete Snobs.* New York: Harper & Row, 1972.
Bird, George L., and Merwin, Frederic E., eds. *The Newspaper and Society: A Book of Readings.* New York: Prentice-Hall, 1942.
Bleyer, Willard Grosvenor. *Main Currents in the History of American Journalism.* Cambridge, Mass.: Houghton Mifflin, 1927.
Chicago Study Team. Report submitted by Daniel Walker, Director of the Chicago Study Team, to the National Commission on the Causes and Prevention of Violence. *Rights in Conflict, The Violent Confrontation of Demonstrators and Police in the Parks and Streets of Chicago During the Week of the Democratic National Convention of 1968.* New York: Grosset & Dunlap, 1968.
Commission on Freedom of the Press. Report of the Commission. *A Free and Responsible Press.* Chicago: University of Chicago Press, 1947.

235

Crawford, Nelson A. *The Ethics of Journalism.* New York: Alfred A. Knopf, 1924.

DeFleur, Melvin L. *Theories of Mass Communication.* 2nd ed. New York: David McKay, 1970.

Duncan, Hugh Dalziel. *Language and Literature in Society.* Chicago: University of Chicago Press, 1953.

Eliot, T. S. *To Criticize the Critic.* New York: Farrar, Straus & Giroux, 1965.

Frye, Northrop. *Anatomy of Criticism.* New York: Atheneum, 1969.

Gerald, J. Edward. *The Social Responsibility of the Press.* Minneapolis: University of Minnesota Press, 1963.

Gross, Gerald, ed. *The Responsibility of the Press.* New York: Simon & Schuster, 1966.

Hachten, William A. *The Supreme Court on Freedom of the Press: Decisions and Dissents.* Ames, Iowa: Iowa State University Press, 1968.

Hearst, William Randolph. *Selections from the Writings and Speeches of William Randolph Hearst.* San Francisco: privately published, 1948.

Hohenberg, John. *Free Press/Free People: The Best Cause.* New York: Columbia University Press, 1971.

Levy, H. Phillip. *The Press Council: History, Procedure and Cases.* New York: St. Martin's Press, 1967.

Lindstrom, Carl E. *The Fading American Newspaper.* Garden City, N.Y.: Doubleday, 1960.

Lippmann, Walter. *The Public Philosophy.* New York: New American Library, 1955.

Lyons, Louis M., ed. *Reporting the News: Selections from Nieman Reports.* New York: Atheneum, 1968.

Mott, Frank Luther. *American Journalism, A History: 1690–1960.* New York: Macmillan, 1962.

Murray, George. *The Press and the Public: The Story of the British Press Council.* Carbondale, Ill.: Southern Illinois University Press, 1972.

National Advisory Commission on Civil Disorders. Report of the Commission. *Report of the National Advisory Commission on Civil Disorders.* New York: Grosset & Dunlap, 1968.

Rivers, William; Blankenburg, William B.; Starck, Kenneth; and Reeves, Earl. *Backtalk.* San Francisco: Canfield Press, 1972.

Rivers, William L., and Schramm, Wilbur. *Responsibility in Mass Communication.* Rev. ed. New York: Harper & Row, 1969.

Seldes, George. *Freedom of the Press.* Garden City, N.Y.: Garden City Publishing, 1937.

Siebert, Fred S.; Peterson, Theodore; and Schramm, Wilbur. *Four Theories of the Press.* Urbana, Ill.: University of Illinois Press, 1963.

Sinclair, Upton. *The Brass Check: A Study of American Journalism.* Pasadena, Calif.: published by the author, 1919.

Tebbel, John. *The Compact History of the American Newspaper.* New York: Hawthorn Books, 1963.

Twentieth Century Fund Task Force. Report of the Task Force for a National News Council. *A Free and Responsible Press.* New York: Twentieth Century Fund, 1973.

Wright, Charles C. *Mass Communications: A Sociological Perspective.* New York: Random House, 1959.

Dissertations and Papers

Blankenburg, William B. "Newspapers' Use of Internal Criticism." American Newspaper Publishing Association, June 1970.

Ferry, W. H., and Ashmore, Harry S. "Mass Communications." The Fund for the Republic, Inc., 1966.

Lowenstein, Ralph L. "Press Councils: Idea and Reality." Freedom of Information Foundation, April 1973.

Midura, Edmund Michael. "An Evaluation of A. J. Liebling's Performance as a Critic of the Press." Ph.D. Dissertation, School of Journalism, University of Iowa, February 1969.

Murray, J. Edward. "The Image of the Newspapers." Speech given at the Associated Press Managing Editors Convention, San Diego, Calif., 18 November 1966.

Sanders, Keith P. "What Are Daily Newspapers Doing to Be Responsive to Readers' Criticisms? A Survey of U.S. Newspaper Accountability Systems." ANPA News Research Center Study, Reston, Va., 30 November 1973.

Periodicals

Barrett, Laurence I. "Monitoring National News Suppliers—Coverage Uneven; Opinion Mixed." *Columbia Journalism Review,* March/April 1973, pp. 53–57.

Blankenburg, William B. "Local Press Councils: An Informal Accounting." *Columbia Journalism Review,* Spring 1969, pp. 14–17.

Bliven, Bruce. "Balance Sheet of American Journalism." *New Republic,* 10 March 1941, pp. 331–34.

Blumberg, Nathan B. "The Press and Its Ineffective Critics." *Nieman Reports*, July 1961, pp. 31–34.

Breed, Warren. "Social Control in the Newsroom." *Social Forces*, May 1955, pp. 326–35.

Brucker, Herbert. "A Conscience for the Press." *Saturday Review*, 9 May 1970, pp. 59–61.

Clayton, Charles C. "Enforceable Code of Ethics." *Grassroots Editor*, July–August 1969, pp. 16–18.

Coren, Marty. "The Perils of Publishing Journalism Reviews." *Columbia Journalism Review*, November/December 1972, pp. 25–48.

Council on Research. "A Plan for the Evaluation of Communication Agencies." *Journalism Quarterly*, December 1948, pp. 395–97.

Harwood, Richard L. "Press Criticism: Who Needs It?" *Bulletin*, American Society of Newspaper Editors, February 1972.

Hausman, Linda Weiner. "Criticism of the Press in U.S. Periodicals, 1900–1939: An Annotated Bibliography." *Journalism Monographs*, August 1967.

Jensen, Jay W. "A Method and a Perspective for Criticism of the Mass Media." *Journalism Quarterly*, Spring 1960, pp. 261–67.

Markel, Lester. "The Real Sins of the Press." *Harper's*, December 1962, pp. 85–94.

Rivers, William L. "Who Shall Guard the Guards?" *Progressive*, September 1971, pp. 23–28.

———. "How to Kill a Watchdog." *Progressive*, February 1973, pp. 44–48.

Rosten, Leo. "The Intellectual and the Mass Media: Some Rigorously Random Remarks." *Daedalus*, Spring 1960, pp. 333–46.

Sexton, William C. "Education for Journalism . . . the Second Century." *Quill*, February 1969, pp. 8–23.

INDEX

239